The Leadership Jigsaw

Transforming Mystery into Mastery

Yemi Akinsiwaju

©2015

The Leadership Jigsaw

Transforming Mystery into Mastery

Yemi Akinsiwaju

Dedication

To my great leader, mentor, friend, teacher, Dr Myles E Munroe. Thank you for living full and leaving empty. Your life was a shining beacon that lit the pathway to leadership greatness anchored in purpose, integrity and love. Your vision of transforming followers into leaders and leaders into agents of positive change continues to live on through the many leaders you raised, nurtured and inspired throughout the world. You are forever loved.

To my precious daughters Oluwaseun, Toluwalope, and Oluwatosin, dare to soar as eagles, release your unique leadership greatness in your generation, and leave a legacy that enriches humanity. I love you!

To you, my esteemed reader… thanks for responding to the clarion call for high quality leadership. I salute you and honour your desire to make our world a better place through your leadership influence… Keep Soaring!

You Have Made A Difference

Thank You

By purchasing this book, you have donated towards enhancing the life of someone in need.

Profits from this book will go towards charitable causes including the work of the following organisations:

Shalom Nagar Lepers Colony:

A place of refuge and life empowerment, run by New Wine International, for lepers and their families in Chennai, India.

Idanre Development Foundation:

Dedicated to fighting poverty, facilitating educational development and raising the quality of life for the underprivileged in Idanre town, Nigeria.

International Third World Leaders Association:

Actively involved in bringing positive change to nations by transforming followers into leaders and leaders into agents of change in over 80 developing countries.

Contents

Foreword

"The most fascinating subject studies over the past 50 years, have been that of leadership. It is my view that the greatest need of the twenty-first century is leadership. Perhaps this is why I am so interested in material like this written by one of my outstanding mentees – Yemi.

This erudite, eloquent, and immensely thought-provoking work gets to the heart of one of the principle challenges of our generation – that of effective and competent leadership.

'*The Leadership Jigsaw*', is indispensable reading for anyone who wants to understand some of the required principles and precepts in our personal development as leaders.

'*The Leadership Jigsaw*' is a profound authoritative research work, which breaks new ground in its approach and will possibly become a classic in this and the next generation as we endeavour to understand the complexities of this seeming illusive subject of leadership.

This exceptional work by Yemi is one of the most profound, practical, principle-centred approaches to this subject I have read for a long time. The author's approach to this timely and very serious issue brings a fresh breath of hope that we can engage the mind, and inspires the spirit of the reader to look at the unique concepts of leadership development and refinement from a different perspective.

The author's ability to leap over complicated metaphysical jargon and reduce complex theories to simple practical principles that the least among us can understand is amazing. This book makes the complicated subject of leadership people-friendly.

This work will challenge the intellectual while embracing the laymen, as it dismantles the mysteries of the soul search of mankind, to develop and exercise sound leadership principles, delivering the profound with simplicity.

Yemi's approach awakens in the reader the untapped possibilities of discovering and developing strategies, to apply to the emerging or experienced leaders in our generation. Also, his antidotes empower us to rise above these self-defeating, self-limiting factors that inhibit our maximizing of our leadership potential.

The author also integrates into each chapter, the research with time-tested precepts giving each principle a practical application to life, making the entire process applicable to any environment.

Every sentence of this book is pregnant with information and I enjoyed the mind-expanding experience of this exciting book. I admonish you to plunge into this ocean of research knowledge and watch your leadership perspective change for the better."

Dr. Myles Munroe
BFM International
Chairman (International Third World Leaders Association – ITWLA)
Nassau, Bahamas

Introduction

Many books have been written on the subject of leadership over the years and the concepts or ideas shared in many of them are still relevant today.

However, the landscape of our world is constantly and rapidly changing and in many countries, we face a new array of challenges. Economic turbulence on a scale never seen before is ravaging many nations such that, almost overnight, the economies of nations are virtually collapsing. Nations like the Republic of Ireland, Iceland, and Greece, which were once heralded as economic success stories are crumbling under the weight of cumulative years of economic mismanagement.

By 2014, the estimated national debt of the United Kingdom was over one trillion pounds and a record 75% of its gross domestic product, whilst the United States of America's national debt was already at 96% of its national output.

Coupled with these economic challenges are the continuing shifts in the political balance of our planet. As America, Japan, and the European nations weaken economically; countries like China, Brazil, India, and Russia that are becoming relatively stronger economically are also emerging as dominant players in the political arena.

Natural disasters are also impacting different areas of our world at such a pace that the question that often arises now is, 'where next?' Within seven months between September 2009 and April 2010, massive earthquakes devastated Haiti, Chile, and China leading to the loss of hundreds of thousands of lives and the displacement of millions. Massive hurricanes and typhoons continue to batter coastal nations, claiming many lives and stifling economic growth.

And then there is the threat of nuclear proliferation as countries like Iran and North Korea pursue the development of their nuclear capabilities.

These global challenges are matched in their potential devastation by the wave of domestic problems bedevilling our nations. Traditional family structures are breaking down at such an alarming rate, that political leaders in many nations have abdicated the responsibility for facing the leadership challenge of effectively rebuilding this foundation of human society.

This breakdown of the family structure is creating awful levels of poverty (children and adults), rising crime, and teenage suicide rates in many urban societies across the world. It has become so bad that the Conservative Party in the United Kingdom referred to the nation as a 'broken society'.

In many Third World countries particularly in Africa and Latin America, these problems are amplified. Famines, corruption in political governance, economic malfeasance, and low scientific and technological capacity continue to exacerbate the terrible standards of living that the citizens have to endure.

The thread that runs through the tapestry of human suffering and agitation described above is the stark manifestation of poor quality leadership in our nations. From Jerusalem, where the mayor is indicted on corruption charges, to China, where major company executives are jailed for bribery of government officials, from Nigeria where presidential aspirants are indicted in the U.S.A for taking bribes from American Halliburton executives, to Iran, where political dissent can cost you your life, effective leadership worth emulating is sadly lacking.

In the domestic arenas, homes are breaking down, predominantly because many men are not living up to their leadership responsibility as fathers and husbands and the same is true of women in their roles as wives and mothers. Furthermore, poorly designed government policies in major western nations actually make it more economically advantageous to break up a family unit.

Education systems are in disarray with a lack of resources, poor performance management or centralised educational bureaucracies often crippling teachers' efforts to teach our children effectively and inculcate in them sound values of character and excellence.

All these, once again reflect the poverty of effective leadership that permeates every level of our societies.

I agree with John Maxwell, the American Leadership philosopher – "Everything rises and falls on leadership."

The Leadership Jigsaw aims to emphasize that we can no longer rely on some political, economic, or other type of leadership 'elite' out there to come up with solutions to the myriad challenges our nations face.

Each one of us needs to respond to the clarion call of leadership in our different arenas of influence and brick by brick, rebuild our homes, communities, and nations with the clear understanding that although we live in our different towns and cities, we are all global citizens of earth and our decisions have interlocking benefits or consequences for all of us.

One of the fascinating things about leadership is that it is like a jigsaw puzzle. Even if you don't know what the full image of a jigsaw puzzle is, you can see clearly when something is missing. Conversely when we have the concrete image of effective leadership and understand the component parts, when you meet a self-proclaimed leader or a pseudo-leader, you can also identify the missing piece.

More importantly however, as we explore this composite image of effective, quality leadership together, continually ask yourself, "Do I have this piece yet? What part do I need to refine? And how will I undertake this refining process, so that I become a more effective and competent leader?"

You can make a positive difference. You have to make a difference. Our world needs you to make a difference. *The Leadership Jigsaw* will share ideas that I hope you choose to adopt or adapt, to your own circumstances as necessary. They will equip you to make that difference, which your family, community, nation, and ultimately our world so badly needs.

I salute your interest and hopefully, commitment to personal leadership growth and hope that in some measure, small or great, *The Leadership Jigsaw* will contribute towards your discovering, enhancing and unleashing your leadership capacity for the benefit of humanity.

Yemi Akinsiwaju

(The Leadership Catalyst)

Know Thyself

Many management development institutions teach courses on leadership, but I have met many of the products of these institutions and found out that they are anything but true leaders.

You may have come across questionnaires that seek to identify personality profiles and leadership capabilities and many organisations use these to assess those whom they think would be suitable to be given the mantle of leadership in their organisations.

A personality profile (also called psychometric test) is a tool used to evaluate an employee's personal skills, traits, and values (such as decision-making methods, management style, communication skills, general attitude towards work and colleagues etc.) with the view to maximizing their job performance.

Yet, those who have emerged from the use of these profiles have become the epitome of dysfunctional leadership that litter the landscape of our businesses, educational establishments, political institutions, and other arenas of human activity.

So, what is the problem?

I believe it stems primarily from the flawed concept of leadership that many people have embraced and that is; 'leadership is about leading others,' and so they go to seminars, leadership schools, and read books on leadership in order to learn techniques and methods that will help them to lead others.

But all that often happens is that such people only learn how to manipulate others to do their bidding and when this does not work, they resort to coercion.

What then is the solution?

It is a return to the core precepts of real leadership found in the following words from an ancient sage:

"He that rules his spirit is better than he who conquers a city."

In essence, true leadership is the product, first of self-mastery. In its purest form, it is the expression of your true self. It is the real you, stripped of pretensions and facades that many put on in order to survive or control the environment in which they exist.

Leadership is an adventure that begins with you. And this sense of wonder and curiosity about unveiling the myriad dimensions that make up the real you, must never cease if you intend to become and remain an effective leader. You simply must, in the enduring words carved upon the walls of Delphi, 'know thyself.'

So let's explore in a bit more depth what this means.

The leader as adventurer

A true leader is on an odyssey of self-discovery. You are on a continual quest to find and refine the answers to the following five key questions of the human heart:

Who am I?

Why am I here?

What can I do?

Where am I from?

Where am I going?

The leader's personal power flows from the answers you obtain to these questions.

'Who am I?'

'Who am I?' is the question of personal identity.

You can't live for too long beyond your perception of yourself. Psychologists and behavioural scientists understand this principle and the multibillion-dollar personal development industry, is built around it.

For many people, their identity is shaped by people's opinions of them or their negative childhood experiences. These often result in an internal struggle that for some, last a lifetime. Why? Because deep in the core of your being, you know that is not who you really are.

Did you embark on a university degree based on someone's opinion of your skill set and your future? Perhaps a parent, teacher, or a school counsellor told you that, "You are excellent in English literature and history but hopeless in maths. You will be better off taking a degree in the arts or social services." Or perhaps you were great in maths and were encouraged to become an accountant.

And so you became trapped by the words of that person. Your university education, your subsequent career, and indeed many years of your life became entombed in the opinions of that person.

And yet, deep within the core of your being, though you have spent the last twenty years working as an accountant, there is a great scientist waiting to be released. Maybe you have been studying and working as a medical doctor all these years, and yet know that your true fulfilment would be found in being a teacher, enriching the lives of young people and helping release them into their own destiny.

You know that just a little more effort in understanding maths or another subject you were supposedly not good at, is all you need to step into your true calling. Or perhaps, it will take a bit more sacrifice, seeing as you have spent so many years sinking deep and deeper into the quicksand of a 'make do' life to break free.

But what will you do...?

Will you go back to work on Monday morning as if you did not just read those last few sentences? I believe they will haunt you from now on until you decide to break free of the casket of the opinions that have held you in the graveyard of self-mediocrity.

Perhaps you have had some very negative experiences as a child or even as an adult and these have moulded you into whom you have become. You might be one of those who proclaim, "I am a realist." by which you really mean you are cynical about the world, untrusting of others and by extension yourself, devoid of a sense of true hope in bringing positive change to our world. Your cynicism has become a layer that you have wrapped around your true self.

The inner spirit within you that is limitless in love, peace, potential, and hope, created in the image or essence of your maker is waiting to be set free.

Everyone goes through some experience that is a shock to the system, which has the potential to create limitations in our lives, and for many people, it manifests itself in their negative reactions to life situations.

The experience may have been public humiliation as a child, abject poverty, rape or incest, racial abuse, physical harm, or some other trauma. The challenge is that too often, this experience is not addressed, and its emotional impact remains unresolved. For some people, attempts to deal with the experience only take them as far as intensifying a victim mentality, which they craft into their identity. You've met them in every walk of life... their mantra is 'bad things always happen to me'.

But it is possible to break free of this contaminated self-identity. Whilst this is not an attempt to proffer medical or psychiatric advice, the following steps have been helpful in liberating many people from the shackles of mental contamination.

- ❖ The first step is to acknowledge that the contamination exists and pinpoint the source.

- ❖ Choose to forgive any other person who was responsible in one way or another, in part or in whole, for what was done to you. If it would help, write a letter of forgiveness to the individual(s) – you don't have to post it.

- ❖ Choose to forgive yourself for your perceived inability to respond adequately at the time of the incident. And forgive yourself for allowing the experience to hold you down for so long.

- ❖ Accept that you are greater than that negative experience.

- ❖ Determine that in your own mind, you will no longer be a victim of that injustice.

- ❖ Then choose each day to live at your new level of freedom.

Some people define their identity as their racial background (Black, White, Asian etc.) or nationality (British, American, Nigerian, Chinese, Jamaican etc.); others define it as their professional career (soldier, doctor, engineer, businesswoman etc.). And some others define themselves as religious labels (bishop, pastor, guru, alhaji, atheist etc.)

However, in talking with many thousands of people over the years and reading extensively on the subject of human potential, I have come to recognise, like many great minds before me, that these identity labels are shallow, misguided, and a disservice to those who use them and the rest of us who have to endure the limitations they impose on you.

The real you, the actual spirit within you, the consciousness within you that is reading these words; is much more than a title or skin colour, or professional label!

You can close your physical eyes and in your mind's eye be standing on top of Mount Everest, walking along the frozen snowy lakes of Alaska, or be driving a jeep through the hot sands of the Sahara desert.

You could close your ears and yet hear within you and compose, just like Beethoven did, a musical symphony of transcendent beauty that enriches the human soul.

You could be deprived of your limbs, but soar in your mind, like Stephen Hawking, the eminent astrophysicist, into space on a quest to decipher the secrets of the universe.

No... My friend, you are much greater than a label slapped on you so that people can categorise you into a filing cabinet of their mind.

You are a gift from the creator to humanity. You are a unique original. There is light within you, which needs to illuminate your corner of this world and we (mankind) need your light to enrich our common experience on this planet.

There has been no one else like you since the dawn of time and there will never be anyone else like you.

YOU ARE THE FIRST AND THE LAST YOU!

And seeing that the creator has taken the time to release this masterpiece called YOU into this universe, the next question you need to confront is why?

Why am I here?

'Why am I here?' relates to the search for personal meaning, the reason for being, i.e. your sense of purpose.

In my book, *Scorecard: Achieving Success and Balance in a Turbulent World*, I enumerated nine key principles of Personal Purpose and the power of a life empowering vision that emanates from understanding those principles.

I will reiterate or add the following in addition to those principles:

a) You were created to fulfil a specific purpose – Of course, if you are of the school of thought that believes that you have inexplicably evolved from some protoplasmic jelly, which itself mysteriously showed up out of nothing, billions of years ago, then life to you is ultimately meaningless... can't help you there!

However, if the idea of your own uniqueness (confirmed by your voice pattern, DNA, fingerprint, retinal eye scan etc.) resonates with you, then it is important to understand that your creator had some important purpose in mind that demanded your showing up on this planet.

b) Where purpose is unknown, the potential for abuse escalates – I'm sure you know from personal experience how true this is. If you hand a lovely, spanking new gadget (mobile phone, camera, or iPad) to your 12-month old son or nephew or friend's baby, does he or she treat it with the same care and love as you do?

No, they drag it on the floor, stomp on it, put it in their mouth, drop it from great heights, and inflict all manner of abuse on your new gadget. The little boy inflicts all this abuse with joy and delight and would even pass the gadget on to other babies around him to inflict the same abuse, all the while oblivious of how you are likely to feel about the matter.

But, the point is this... these children are not being malicious, they simply do not know the purpose of that iPad and abuse (abnormal use) is virtually inevitable, unless there is intervention to rescue your gadget.

This scenario holds true for many millions of lives on this planet. Until you get a glimpse of your purpose, life remains an experiment in futility and a candidate for self-abuse or abuse by others. Unfortunately for many, this experiment or abuse lasts a lifetime and is reflected in the plethora of unfulfilling jobs, discordant relationships, dysfunctional spirituality, and poor physical health choices.

You owe it to yourself as a leader to discover and pursue the fulfilment of your purpose, thus protecting yourself from self-abuse and abuse by others.

c) Your purpose is encoded within you – Like the purpose of an apple seed, which is to bring forth an apple, is encoded within itself, so your personal purpose is hard-coded into you.

One of my criticisms of the 'personal development movement' is the idea that 'you can be whatever you want to be.' That, in my view, is absolute nonsense!

You cannot be ***whatever*** you want to be… such frivolous thinking is the continuing pathway to frustration.

A gorilla trying to fly like a bird may launch itself from a mountaintop of euphoria and positive self-talk, and indeed it may seemingly fly for a while, but the ultimate direction and destination is downwards and an encounter with pain.

A gorilla is not designed to fly. Its purpose is to be a powerful influencer in the jungle, and if you meet one fulfilling its purpose in its natural environment, you know what wisdom dictates!

Similarly, whilst you cannot be *whatever* you want to be, you can be ***everything*** you were designed, wired, born, and purposed to be… a tremendous leader in a particular area of gifting, ability, or strength, flowing gracefully in your purpose.

Your responsibility is to discover this unique purpose and manifest its greatness… Therein lies your leadership.

d) Effective living only begins when you accept the responsibility for fulfilling your purpose – I believe that discovery of personal purpose is a crucial first step in maximised living, but in far too many cases, all it remains is a discovery.

To be the leader you were born to be, you must step beyond discovery to accept that you have been entrusted with a great responsibility.

The precious seed of purpose that you are carrying within you will need to be planted in the right environment, properly nurtured, trimmed, and pruned as necessary, allowed to blossom fully and then it will bring forth fruit that honours the giver of the seed and blesses the partaker of the fruit.

That responsibility for discovering your purpose and fulfilling it is yours and no one else's. Until your whole being resonates with the true answer to the question of, "Why am I here?" you merely exist. And until you can say "YES... for this, I was born." then step into this river of destiny, you are depriving humanity of the best you have to offer.

You are robbing you; your family, your nation, and this planet, of the truly maximised gift of one of its greatest assets – the real you.

Where am I from?

This is often interpreted as a question about nationality or ethnic origin, but in the context of effective leadership, it is a much deeper question.

As we already alluded to earlier, there is a part of you that transcends the physical dimensions of time and space. In the quiet moments, perhaps when you are by yourself, sitting beside a calm lake or gazing quietly at the stars in the night, this is a question that lies at the heart of the origin of your spirit or consciousness.

It is a question that will continually intrude upon your thoughts, seeking an answer that resonates with your sense of true self.

Any objective quest for this answer will ultimately lead you to the simple truth that you are more than a protoplasmic accident. You are a phenomenal product of the mind of God (the Infinite being or original source of every living thing), created to manifest some part of His essence in a way that nobody else really could.

Where am I going?

Many have sought to answer this question and have arrived at different conclusions. My perception of this question is not about a physical destination, but about accountability for your actions.

Everyone is ultimately accountable to someone. When all is said and done, to whom are you accountable for all that you have done, with all that you have been given, whilst you sojourned on this planet?

This question is particularly critical for leaders who are at the very top of their organisation, perhaps as CEO, President, Pastor, King, Pope, Prime Minister etc. Also, those who wield great influence as thought leaders e.g. entertainers, sports personalities, musicians etc. would benefit from asking themselves this question.

Whilst you may wield authority that makes it difficult for your immediate followers to hold you to account, I encourage you to keep this question at the forefront of your thinking. You must understand that your power, no matter how great it presently is, is temporal and you will have to give an account to the one (s) who entrusted you with such power. If not here on earth, then it will be to the ultimate giver of your leadership gift – your creator.

This understanding should help a leader live a life of balance, which helps them avoid the trap of intoxicating power that corrupts and leads to abuse. A leadership sense of accountability will enable you to lead with compassion those who follow you.

What can I do?

You are an embodiment of gifts, creative ideas, abilities, and passions, which all converge into what we call your potential.

Knowing yourself includes a careful analysis of all those innate abilities you possess. Endeavour never to discount the value of any gift you have. Something that you take for granted is the solution someone else desperately needs to enhance their own life.

I am inspired by the story of Nicholas James Vujicic, born with Tetra-amelia syndrome, a rare disease characterised by the absence of all four limbs.

As a result of his disability, Nick had a difficult childhood, suffering bullying from his schoolmates, and even contemplating suicide at one point.

However, he looked beyond his disabilities to ask the question, "What can I do?" and his response to this question has taken him to over 24 countries on five continents as a motivational speaker, inspiring over three million people in schools, churches, personal development events, and corporate audiences.

His book, *Life Without Limits: Inspiration for a Ridiculously Good Life* is a testament to the truth that, whatever your present circumstances, you are endowed with tremendous potential and you can do so much with this gift of life that you possess.

As a leader, ask yourself this 'potential' question regularly, because it could serve as the catalyst that propels you forward into each new level of effectiveness and productive living.

Remember, the leader is an adventurer and the journey of self-discovery is a never-ending one for the leader who is committed to internal mastery, and longevity in their leadership influence.

Know Thyself – Interactive Exercise

What are your responses to the following questions?

Who am I? (What is your personal identity? How did you arrive at this identity? And does it truly capture who you really are?)

_____

_____

_____

Why am I here? (Have you discovered your purpose? What is it?)

_____

_____

_____

What can I do? (Have you taken an inventory of all your abilities, gifts, or talents? What could you do with them that you're not currently doing, and why?)

_____

_____

_____

Where am I from? (What do you think is the source of your uniqueness? How does this influence you as a leader?)

_____

_____

_____

Where am I going? (To whom are you accountable? How do you practice accountability?)

_____

_____

_____

What other questions arise for you from this section?

_____

_____

_____

What will you do in response to these additional questions?

_____

_____

_____

Vision

Vision is the ability to see. In the field of optics, natural sight is dependent on three key factors: a source of light, an object, and the human eye. The diagram below is a simple representation of the process of seeing.

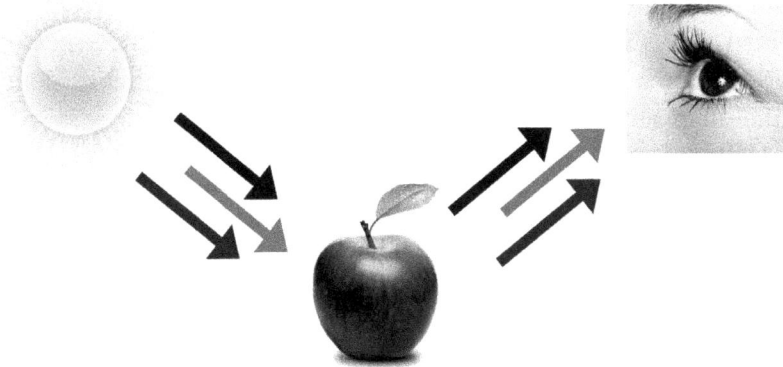

The light shines on the object and from the object; it is reflected to the eyeball. When the reflected light reaches the eye, it is processed through a vast array of nerve endings, the neural network, and the brain which then interprets the information received as the object. And all of this is done within a fraction of a second.

If any of the components involved in the process of seeing is changed in any way, the outcome is also altered.

For example, change the light or source of illumination, e.g. from bright sunlight to infrared light only and this affects what you see, even if the object has not physically changed. Dim the lights available and this impacts your ability to see the object clearly.

Change the eyes that receive the light from the object and this again impacts on the vision. This is why corrective surgery and other forms of eye treatment exist today to help address health problems with the eye.

And of course, if you change the object that the eyes focus on, what you see is again different.

Finally, it is important to emphasise that the eventual outcome of the physical act of seeing, depends on how you interpret what your eyes behold, which in turn depends on your personal frame of reference. So one man sees a snake and based on his frame of reference (personal experience or other source of knowledge), interprets this as danger. Another man sees the same snake and sees it as a pet.

Just as this is true for natural sight, it is also true for inner sight, or what we call 'vision' as it relates to leadership. Your vision is the interpretation of the possibilities of all that which your heart (otherwise called your inner eyes) beholds. Sometimes it is referred to as your dream or your aspirations for a better future.

One man looks at a block of granite and ignores it as a worthless entity. Another man, a leader in the art of sculpting, looks at the same block of granite and sees within it a beautiful sculpture of a war hero on his horse.

One man looks at a lady and only sees a plaything for the night. Another man, a real leader, sees a creature of dignity, beauty, and intelligence, worthy of respect and honour.

You and other people may be looking at the same thing, but as a leader, what are you seeing?

Vision is a critical component of effective leadership. As Dr Myles Munroe points out, "Leadership depends on capturing, refining, planning, simplifying, documenting, communicating, living, and maintaining a noble vision." [1]

Seeing that it is important to our effectiveness as leaders, how do we develop and maintain optimum vision?

By paying attention to all the requisite components identified in our simple diagram above:

1. The source of illumination

2. The objects we focus on

3. The eyes with which we see

1. Illumination: In leadership terms, this refers to the sources of knowledge and ideas that you allow to illuminate your mind. These can be in the form of books, music, teachers, or other forms of input that shape your intellectual or philosophical development.

All human activity begins with an idea. When an idea takes root and is allowed to flourish, it can cast its glow over every aspect of a person's life and effectively shapes his or her vision of the future.

As an example, communism and capitalism are ideas originating from someone's mind. Depending on which idea you choose to embrace, this source of illumination colours virtually everything else that you 'see.'

As a leader therefore, it is critical that you carefully select, monitor, and control the sources of ideas that illuminate your mind. As General Colin Powell once stated, "Ideas matter; Ideas build up or bring down empires."

2. The object: You may have heard the maxim, 'what you focus on expands.' This is particularly true in respect of your vision as a leader.

There are millions of 'objects' or ideas to focus on and much of them are a distraction from what your life really is about. So the question becomes, "What should I focus on?" The answer lies in your sense of personal purpose. Once you have discovered purpose, clarity of vision becomes your powerful reality, because your vision becomes the visual representation of that purpose, which you have captured.

Focus your mind and energies on the fulfilment of that vision (your object) and your leadership capabilities will emerge.

What if you have still not discovered your purpose? Then I suggest that you find another leader who has discovered their purpose and vision, and test whether supporting their journey resonates with you. If it does, align yourself with the vision as you work towards discovering your purpose and clarifying your vision. Then you should focus on making that leader's vision a success.

Note of caution… never let this become a permanent detour from finding and fulfilling your own life purpose.

3. Your 'eye': In this case, we are not referring to your physical organ for seeing, but to your internal mechanism for processing the inputs that enter your mind i.e. your mental vision. It is a composite of your thinking ability and your attitude.

Your willingness to think clearly and objectively is a necessity for effective leadership. Presumptuous action without meticulous thought, has been the downfall of many a leader. Many wars, business failures, and moral deficiencies have been traced back to deficient thinking by someone in a leadership position. Please do not be numbered amongst such leaders, who refuse to cultivate the right thinking and who eventually end up in the refuse dump of history.

If you have a positive, optimistic attitude about life, it affects how you 'see' the different experiences and circumstances you encounter.

Indeed it also influences your capacity to take advantage of those opportunities that life brings your way.

Your attitude as a leader will attract or repel people, resources, and opportunities that you need to fulfil any noble endeavour you desire.

And just as corrective treatment is required to improve your physical eyes if your natural sight is impaired, corrective action needs to be taken when your mental vision is impaired. Such corrective action can include the following:

❖ Reading the right books that enrich your psyche with wholesome input

❖ Attending a church that inspires your growth and empowers your faith

❖ Listening to uplifting music and material with a positive life-enriching message

❖ Attending high quality personal development seminars to learn from other good leaders

❖ Minimising or eliminating the time spent watching noxious television programmes

❖ Investing quality time with great leaders who mentor you and challenge you to grow

As a leader, you have the responsibility for protecting your vision. No one else can do it for you. Remember that your vision is your personal interpretation of the limitless possibilities of your own life, and of what you would want your contributions to human history to be.

Vision, in its truest sense, is not merely seeing; it is living. It is living… in the now, in a way that leads to the fulfilment of the 'dream' you saw.

There are three important benefits of a noble vision that make it worthwhile for any current or aspiring leader to have one.

Vision contextualises your past: What this means is that a worthy vision enables you to develop a positive perspective of the events of your past. It helps you to realise that everything that has happened to you up until this very moment, has shaped who you are. Nothing in your past is superfluous; positive or negative, there are lessons you can extract from those experiences for use in the present and in the future.

If you have had negative experiences in the past, your story can serve as the means of inspiration to others on how to develop a winner's mindset. For example, I remember sitting in a seminar at which Lord Alan Sugar, a highly successful British entrepreneur and TV personality (The Apprentice) shared the story of his upbringing and the abject poverty in his childhood, as he grew up in the East End of London in England.

His poverty experience served as his catalyst to build his businesses and breakthrough into wealth. His vision of a wealthy future enabled him to use the poverty of his past as fuel for personal motivation.

And of course, the lessons of those past struggles that he shared, inspired many people in that seminar room to believe that they could succeed too.

Vision empowers your present: Having a powerful dream of a better future makes you almost invincible to the challenges that naturally come with the quest to succeed. When your heart is focussed on a noble vision, you develop a mindset that says, "This challenge is temporary... it shall pass."

Whatever your current circumstances, it is important to maintain a focus on your aspirations for the future. Present day problems can often seem so intractable that unfortunately, some have caved in and taken their own lives, thinking there was no way out.

There is **ALWAYS** a way out. Failure is never final. Out of the ashes of failure, victory can, and often does emerge, to the surprise of many who had perhaps written you off.

Just ask the following people:

❖ Abraham Lincoln – Legendary president of the United States of America

❖ Donald Trump – Billionaire real estate mogul

❖ Toni Braxton – Grammy award-winning songstress

❖ Larry King – Celebrated American TV personality and host of the Larry King Show

❖ Walt Disney – Founder of the world famous Disney cartoon characters and associated products and services

All of these people suffered financial bankruptcy and yet emerged from this experience to go on to achieve greater success in life.

What about Oprah Winfrey, the billionaire chat show hostess whose *Oprah Winfrey* show remained at the top of the ratings charts for much of the twenty-five years that it ran. Did you know that before her success, she was fired from her job as a television reporter because she was deemed 'unfit for television'?

So, each day you wake up, let your noble vision empower you and energise you to be the best that you can be for the day, knowing that you are laying the foundations for your more glorious future.

Vision clarifies your future: A noble vision acts as a magnet that attracts you onwards and upwards towards your future. It also clarifies the activities that will get you there.

For example, if you desire to be a successful Olympic athlete, it is clear that you will require a focussed regime of mental, dietary, and physical discipline. You simply cannot eat, drink, and smoke whatever you want, whenever you want. The vision of Olympic success makes demands on you that are non-negotiable.

There is always a price to pay for any vision you want to accomplish and this brings clarity on what you can and cannot do or what you must or must not do.

Such clarity is necessary in helping you to channel your physical, intellectual, and spiritual energies in the right direction.

Having established the benefits of having a noble vision, what is required to translate your vision from simply remaining a dream to its becoming a reality?

Document your vision: An ancient sage once wrote, "Write the vision down. Make it plain upon tablets that he who reads it may run."

You must capture your vision in writing. Sometimes the vision starts off hazy in your mind's eye. Writing it down, enables you to refine, clarify and articulate it effectively.

Writing helps to crystallize your thoughts and reduce misconceptions. One of the ways in which your vision can also be documented is in the use of vision boards.

A vision board is simply a visual representation of the dreams that you have in your heart. It is a collage or collection of pictures that depict the things that you are aiming to accomplish. For example if your vision is to build a hospital to help Third World children overcome the challenges of poor health facilities in their nations, put up a picture of a hospital on your board.

If it is to become an Olympic gold medallist, you may want to put up a picture of a winning Olympian, with the face replaced with yours (you can be as creative as you like…)

Then ensure you put your board in a place where you can regularly review it and update it if need be.

Nowadays, there is software that enables you to create a vision board on your computer and use the collage of images as your screensaver. Or you can also set your collage of images to music in a home-made movie, using basic computer-based software.

All of these can be a powerful tool, in always keeping your vision before you.

Turn it into a magnificent obsession: Until your dream becomes an obsession, it is unlikely that you will accomplish it. No great champion of life ever sleepwalked into the fulfilment of their vision.

A noble vision will demand all that you have to offer and then some more. That is why it must be anchored in your personal purpose; the assignment for which you were born carries within it an intrinsic fire that lights you up each time you think about it.

A number of ways to stoke the fire of your vision include:

❖ Look at your documented vision regularly. Whether it's in writing or whether you use a physical or computer-based vision board, look at your vision regularly. Especially during times of difficulty, look at your documented vision even more frequently. This will help you maintain commitment to your vision when your circumstances are screaming at you to give up.

It is simply a vital requirement for your success; your vision has to become your passion.

❖ Visualize your success. Regularly take a mental journey to preview your future. Many studies in the field of superlative performance have attested to the power of visualization. Find some space each week to spend time alone and visualize yourself achieving your dreams and goals.

There is an abundance of information available on effective visualization techniques. It is definitely worth your while to explore this subject and develop this skill properly. When used correctly, visualisation will infuse you with renewed passion for your dreams.

Connect with the right mentor: This is one of the most important decisions you can make in your life as a current or aspiring leader. When you read the biographies of many of the successful people in current or past history, you will notice a recurring theme... they trace much of their success to the impact of a mentor on their lives.

- ❖ Nelson Mandela, one of the greatest leaders in contemporary human history and former president of South Africa had Walter Sisulu as his political mentor.

- ❖ Bill Clinton, the former president of the U.S.A had Virgil Spurlin, his high school band director as his mentor.

- ❖ Margaret Thatcher, the first female prime minister of the United Kingdom, was mentored by Sir Keith Joseph, a British cabinet minister.

- ❖ Vladimir Putin, the two-time President of Russia was mentored by the former president, Boris Yeltsin

- ❖ Michael Jordan, the legendary basketball player was mentored by his coach, Phil Jackson.

- ❖ Celine Dion, the music megastar who has sold over 200 million albums worldwide was mentored by her manager and future husband, Rene Angelil.

The right mentor will see the greatness in you and hold you accountable to your vision. He or she will be committed to your future and will not let you get off with silly excuses as to why you have not made progress towards the noble dreams and worthy accomplishments that you are capable of achieving.

Effective leaders who have left a lasting impact are characterised by an unrelenting focus on a vision they have captured, documented, reviewed regularly, and pursued vigorously.

Vision – Interactive Exercise

What is your vision? (Is it properly documented and reviewed regularly?) Write a one-sentence version of your vision here.

_____

_____

_____

Do you pursue your vision vigorously? (List here the key things that you have done in the last six months in actively pursuing your vision and the results you have achieved.)

_____

_____

_____

Is anything sabotaging your vision? (What is it? How does it affect you?)

_____

_____

_____

Do you have the right vision enablers? (Mentors – Who are they? Visualisation tools/routine – what are they?)

_____

_____

_____

What other questions arise for you from this section?

_____

_____

_____

What will you do in response to these additional questions?

_____

_____

_____

Innovation

Innovation is a product of vision. It is simply doing something different because you 'see' differently from others – It can be big or small. Innovation is not a one-off happenstance event of doing something; it is more of a cultivated disposition towards positive, ongoing change, leading towards the fulfilment of a predetermined vision.

To be successful as an innovative leader, it is important to give some consideration to the following:

Innovation requires thinking – One of the most powerful examples of innovation is the highly respected technology company, Apple. Their motto is, 'Think different' and that in a nutshell captures the power behind successful innovation… thinking.

As a leader, strive to create and maintain an environment that stimulates creative thinking, both for yourself and for your team.

I remember speaking recently to a proud father whose child had graduated from primary school, top of her class, and with results that placed her in the top five percent of primary school pupils in the country. He told me that his daughter always had tremendous potential for great results, but in her earlier years in school, she was falling behind in her studies. He explored ways of reversing this problem and arrived at a deceptively simple solution.

They agreed that his daughter would not watch television in the morning before ten o'clock. The time between her waking up and going-to-school would be turned to 'thinking time,' that would allow his daughter to calm her mind, focus her thoughts, and prepare for her day… this small change in his daughter's daily routine yielded big results in her educational attainment.

If you find that your life is so frantic that you never have time for regular deep, quality thinking, you are seriously impairing your capacity for innovation and this will eventually reveal itself in the mediocre results you produce. Just as this is true for you personally, it is also true for any team or organisation that you lead.

The power of critical observation – In the words of Arthur Schopenhauer: "The task is not so much to see what no one has yet seen, but to think what nobody yet has thought about that which everybody sees."

Many physical inventions trace their origins to the power of observation. Someone looked at a mistake or some other common human experience; analysed their observation critically and 'saw' the same situation from a different perspective.

For example, the ubiquitous Post-it notes have become a critical piece of stationery in many offices around the world. It is a piece of paper with a strip of adhesive on its back that enables the paper to stick to many types of surfaces. The adhesive was originally developed by Spencer Silver, a scientist with the company called 3M, in 1968.

He promoted this adhesive within his company without much success for five years and nobody saw its possible benefits. Then one of his colleagues, Art Fry thought differently about that which everyone else had seen. Art applied the adhesive to a piece of stationery for use as a bookmark and the Post-it notes were born. Through a series of refinements and developments, Post-it has become a global brand enjoyed by millions around the world.

This concept of observation is also tied closely to listening. Many ideas that have revolutionised the 21st century have come from businesses that listened intently to their clients. Indeed customer relationship management (which encompasses handling complaints) is a critical element of business success today, because it helps an organisation identify what it is doing wrong, or even what it is doing right but could do better.

As a leader, listen to all stakeholders (i.e. everyone who has a vested interest in you, your endeavours, or your success. Depending on your context, this may include family, friends, employees, customers, colleagues, community etc.). This will provide you with a wealth of knowledge about their passions, aspirations, and expectations that can all serve as the foundation for innovative products and services.

The key is to listen effectively to gain useful knowledge, and based on the insight gleaned from your stakeholders' experiences, design and produce solutions that transform their source of complaints into positive experiences.

So, what 'problems' are you observing in your immediate environment? And what critical thinking are you bringing to your observations? You just may be on the verge of producing a solution that our world so dearly needs.

Innovation thrives in a culture of curiosity – As a leader of a family, small team or large business, the size of the innovation unit doesn't really matter, it is your responsibility to foster a culture of curiosity or exploration within your team. Such a culture arises from continually asking the following questions:

❖ Why do we do things this way?

❖ How can we do it differently?

And don't be afraid of the answers you will receive or the direction in which such creative thinking will take you... You may find that the new direction will actually take you to your destination much faster.

Challenge the status quo – A true leader is not content to rest on yesterday's excellence. They understand that there is no gear called 'neutral' in this vehicle called life. When you ask the question, "Why do we do it like this?" and you get the response, "We've always done it like this." or some other variant of this response, you know it is time to bring out the big guns and go to war against stagnation and mediocre thinking.

Such a response is a clear indication that the respondent or the organisation that they represent has become trapped in a mental rut that will sooner or later result in the decline or demise of the organisation.

Innovation demands courage and as a leader, you must be willing to challenge the status quo and encourage critical analysis of all facets of personal or organisational activity.

As a business consultant, I have found that the barriers to innovation in many organisations are often middle managers or senior executives who are caught up in politicking and fighting turf wars, to the detriment of the organisation.

Many junior members of staff understand what is wrong with their organisations and how to fix it, especially at the points where the organisation interfaces with the customers. However, many of their innovative ideas are lying on the shop floor gathering dust because no one has bothered to engage their creativity effectively.

As a true leader, you can energise your team, department, or company by returning to your team, picking their ideas off the shop floor, dusting them off, and empowering your staff to implement them. You will be amazed at the increased productivity this will generate within your organisation. Innovation demands that you be courageous… Are you?

Resilience in the face of criticism – You will have some failures and this will provide cannon fodder for the small-minded to criticise you. But you cannot allow this to stop you.

Also, the outcomes of innovation are new and oftentimes, people fear or misunderstand new ideas or products. Hence they may attack you. In the words of Eva LaGallienne, "Innovators are inevitably controversial." [2]

Provided the motive for the innovation is for the benefit of humanity and does not infringe on the rights of others, remain steadfast in your focus on innovation. Have the courage to ignore unfounded criticism.

Innovation demands an appetite for risk – The fear of failure ranks at the top of many people's fears and unfortunately this leads to intellectual atrophy and diminished results. When this fear is coupled with an environment where mistakes are harshly criticised or penalised, it is no wonder that your people are unwilling to risk failure, to risk being misunderstood, or to risk suffering criticism, and hence innovation is stifled.

Therefore, to be an effective, innovative leader, you must give yourself permission to fail and you should allow your team members the freedom to fall on their faces once in a while, whilst exploring new approaches. Mistakes are the fertilizer for the tree of success. Allow yourself and others to grow through and beyond your mistakes.

By all means, create a framework within which innovative ideas can be tested (e.g. time commitments, budget restrictions or other resource guidelines), but you have to eradicate the fear of failure. Let your people know that failure is not final and as history has shown us repeatedly, grand success has often been the phoenix that arises out of the ashes of spectacular failure.

Innovation requires patience and long-term thinking – In our 21st century world built on instant gratification, patience is a virtue that is required if you are to be successful in innovation. Why? Because your idea may suffer several false starts or repeated failures before it finally materialises into the glowing success that you dreamed of. Thomas Edison reportedly attempted up to ten thousand different experiments before finally arriving at his answer for creating the light bulb. His patience and persistence paid off and it will for you too.

Ignore the experts sometimes – An interesting reality TV programme aired on BBC television in England is called the Dragon's Den. In this programme, budding entrepreneurs seek funding for their enterprise by making a pitch to a number of seasoned, successful businessmen and women who decide whether the product or service is worth investing in.

Sometimes these business experts unanimously conclude (often with quite acidic comments) that a business idea has absolutely no chance of being successful. But again and again and again, they are proved wrong. Some of the products that were turned down went on to become great commercial success stories... Just ask Rob Law, the founder of Trunki, who produced luggage especially designed for children.

Oren Harari stated, "A leader affords the pros their dignity but he is fully prepared to assert that the pros can be wrong." This is a sentiment with which I wholeheartedly agree.

Henry Ford, the legendary founder of the Ford Motor Company in his quest to build the Ford V-8 engine in one block, was repeatedly told by the automotive experts of his day that this was impossible. He disregarded their opinion and maintained his commitment to see this dream fulfilled. Eventually they found a way to build the engine and this radically transformed his company's fortunes. In addition, this feat catapulted the entire motor industry into a new level of innovation and development.

So, as an innovative leader, be willing to challenge conventional thinking and have the courage of your convictions even when faced with the daunting opinions of so-called experts.

As stated earlier, innovation can be small or big. And it comes via different routes. It can be something completely original or it could simply be a combination of old ideas in fresh ways.

A well-known method for stimulating innovative ideas is the **SCAMPER** model developed by Robert Eberle. The word is an acronym that identifies different approaches to creativity in the development of products or services.

> **S – Substitute**: Could you substitute materials or components that make up your current product or service? Or perhaps you could substitute the people who are responsible for specific functions or who deliver the service. For example in the world of sport, substitutions are often the little things that make a huge difference to the results of a game. Substitution could be the decisive method you need to transform your results as a leader.
>
> **C – Combine**: Are you able to improve productivity or accelerate your results by combining with other functions or including additional elements? It may be that you need to combine your efforts with those of another person or organisation to generate exponential success.
>
> **A – Adapt**: This seeks to answer the question, "What can I adapt or copy from someone else?" It might even be something that seemingly failed elsewhere. Do you remember the Post-it notes story I mentioned earlier?
>
> **M – Modify**: You can alter the shape, colour, texture, taste, or other attribute of your product. Soft drinks manufacturers excel in this practice of modifying taste or colour to create new flavours.
>
> Think about what you offer and identify where simple changes in the attributes could bring positive benefits. You could even modify yourself! If your leadership arena is health and wellness, you may find that your credibility is dramatically enhanced if

you modify your physical appearance through wiser dietary habits and a healthy exercise regime.

P – Put to another use: As an example, the braking system used in aeroplanes has been put to another use in Formula 1 racing cars. Think laterally about multiple uses for the same product or service. Or in the words of internet marketers, think always about 'repurposing.'

E – Eliminate: Remove anything unnecessary; simplify or reduce to core requirements. Sometimes, your clients or stakeholders just want simplicity and superfluous additions reduce their enjoyment of your product or service.

As a leader who is committed to innovation, don't be afraid to streamline and eliminate anything that does not definitively add value to your life or to your interactions with your stakeholders. By the way, this could mean removing negative, energy-sapping people from your inner circle.

R – Reverse: This is about turning things inside out or upside down. Whereas most innovations often lead to incremental change, 'reverse' innovations are often radical, discontinuous changes. Sometimes, this is what it takes to kick-start a person or organisation that has remained in stagnation for too long.

Not only will the application of this model for innovative thinking benefit you personally, sharing the methodology with your team and facilitating an environment in which they can readily apply its principles, will yield great results in innovation and productivity.

In the words of Steve Jobs, the quintessential expression of technological innovation and co-founder of Apple Inc., "Innovation distinguishes between a leader and a follower."

Innovation – Interactive Exercise

Do you consider yourself to be innovative? (If YES, how are you innovative? If NO, why are you not?)

_____

_____

_____

Do you encourage innovation within your sphere of influence? (If YES, how are you doing so? If NO, why are you not? And what are the results of your choice?)

_____

_____

_____

What innovative ideas have you implemented in the last six months? (List them here and the results.)

_____

_____

_____

What innovative ideas will you implement in the next six months?
(List them here and the anticipated outcomes.)

_____

_____

_____

Which elements of the SCAMPER model could/would you apply in the next six months?
(In which area of your work or life could you/would you apply them?)

_____

_____

_____

What other questions arise for you from this section?

_____

_____

_____

What will you do in response to these additional questions?

_____

_____

_____

Responsibility

A little while back, after I finished speaking at an event, one of the delegates approached me to have a chat. As our conversation developed, he asked my advice about how to handle some problems he was experiencing with his new boss, and also let slip that he had passed up the opportunity to become the manager of the team, of which he was now a part.

I asked him why he had not taken the opportunity to lead the team, which would have helped to avoid the problems he was complaining about. His answer was quite revealing; he said, "I don't like the pressure, stress or responsibility of being the boss."

That response highlights a critical problem that keeps many people from stepping up to becoming the leader they could be… a demonstrable lack of a sense of responsibility.

Fathers abscond from their homes and avoid taking responsibility for the children they helped bring into the world. Parents, instead of accepting their responsibility for moulding the character of their children, blame teachers for their children's poor behaviour. Government ministers, rather than accept responsibility for the poor performances of their departments, regularly shift blame and responsibility onto the shoulders of their hapless subordinates.

And of course many citizens, rather than accept the responsibility to contribute actively towards the development of their communities, and influence the change they want to see, sit instead in front of their televisions for hours on end, watching and criticising those who, at least are trying to do something.

Because you are reading this book, I believe you are not one of those people who refuse to take responsibility. You have determined that you will be an agent of transformation and this book will equip you with some of the tools to do so.

Before we delve into some of the key responsibilities required of effective leaders, let us explore a number of elements that have led to this crisis of a lack of responsibility.

You don't need to have all the answers

There is often the mistaken belief that the leader has to be the smartest person in the group, with all the answers to every situation. If that false notion is keeping you from leadership, let me assure you that such a notion is a complete falsehood. Indeed the experiences of many followers have proven how ludicrous such an idea is. You have probably met some so-called leader who was foolish enough to think that they had all the answers and yet you knew (wink, wink), based on their results, that they did not.

One of the key characteristics of great leaders is the humility to recognise that they do not have all the answers and a willingness to celebrate others who do have the answers that they lack.

Remember that your leadership is a function of your own unique capabilities. Combine this with a sincere desire to work collaboratively with other people and you will find that leadership does not have to be as stressful as you imagined; you can therefore approach leadership with a willingness to accept responsibility, simply as one who is first among equals.

Responsibility is not about position

In many organisations, the person who carries the leadership title or occupies the position of authority is oftentimes not the real leader. Why – because real leadership is not about the position.

The word 'responsibility' draws on two other words: response and ability. If you have the ability, whether it is physical, intellectual, moral, or otherwise to respond effectively to a situation, then life is offering you an invitation to leadership.

If you do not respond appropriately, the outcome generally is that someone else who is less effective will attempt to fill the gap either because of ignorance or ambition. This in turn leads to a scenario where this 'second choice' pseudo-leader struggles to lead, he is perennially stressed and the organisation or other stakeholders (anyone who experiences the impact of the poor leadership) consequently suffer... all because the true leader was afraid to step up and take responsibility.

Responsibility is about the willingness to contribute actively; to be the solution to a problem or the answer to an important question your stakeholders are asking. And you do not require a title or a position to contribute.

Feel the fear and do it anyway

When you observe some of the pressures that leaders endure, it is understandable that some people might become fearful of taking up the mantle of leadership. Such people are afraid of making wrong decisions, afraid of being criticised, afraid of being held accountable and this fear maintains a stranglehold on their leadership potential, some for a lifetime... But it does not have to be so.

Yes, people may misunderstand and criticise you and yes, you will make some wrong decisions, but you don't have to allow the fear of these to hold you back. In the words of Susan Jeffers, you can feel the fear and do it anyway. Suffice to say that you will be in great company; all the great leaders in human history have experienced the same fear at some point in their lives, have overcome them and gone on to achieve great things. You can do the same and accept the responsibility to become the leader you were born to be.

A number of key demands that are incumbent upon you as an effective leader include the following:

1. Responsible delegation

I use the term 'responsible delegation' because I have seen many a leader handle delegation so poorly that it could only be described as being irresponsible.

Delegation is generally thought of as a way to improve the leader's productivity by farming out tasks to others, especially subordinates within the organisational context. The challenge of course is that by farming out the tasks, it often becomes 'out of sight is out of mind.' Furthermore, the delegation of the task is treated as the abdication of the responsibility for that task.

This explains why, like I mentioned earlier, state ministers would rather blame their long-suffering civil servants for things that have gone wrong in their departments; or managers would choose to blame their staff for work projects that have gone awry. This is the hallmark of irresponsibility.

In contrast, responsible delegation has the following characteristics:

❖ The true leader never abdicates responsibility for work they have delegated to others.

❖ You carefully select the right person for the right task, bearing in mind that the choice of who you delegate tasks to, sends some clear signals to all those who are watching. I share more about this shortly.

❖ The leader maintains a watchful eye over everything delegated and has an effective mechanism for monitoring and evaluating performance.

❖ The leader does not set others up for failure by delegating tasks to them that they are incapable of fulfilling properly.

❖ The leader sincerely shares the credit for success with as many contributors as possible.

❖ The true leader does not play the blame game. The buck stops with them.

When you practise responsible delegation, you communicate some very potent signals to your organisation.

❖ You signal that you are keen to maximise your own productivity, hence releasing your time and effort to undertake those tasks that yield the greatest results from your input.

❖ You communicate that you recognise what you are best at and the areas in which you add the greatest value to your organisation.

❖ You signal that you are humble enough to accept that others are better than you at some tasks and you are willing to let them handle those activities.

❖ You show that you are willing to share the credit for the success of your ventures/activities.

❖ You signal your confidence in the ability of the person to whom you delegate. This enhances their confidence and reinforces their commitment to your objectives even further.

❖ You communicate to all stakeholders the quality of conduct, attitude, and performance that earns your trust, respect, and reward.

❖ You send the message that you are on the lookout for rising stars who you want to develop into leaders.

❖ You signal that you are keen to develop your team by giving them more responsibility for results (although you still retain overall responsibility).

❖ You are also providing practical training to your team or organisation in how to delegate responsibly and effectively.

2. Be the 'Chief Inspiration Officer'

The leader has the responsibility for creating and maintaining the right morale or inspiring environment for the vision to flourish. Empirical research has shown that maintaining positive morale in the workplace is not just some fuzzy social scientist's idea. It has a demonstrable, practical impact on the productivity of an organisation and the financial results of a business.

This is just as true in other environments including our homes, non-profit organisations, churches, sports clubs, or any other gathering of humans you can think of; inspiration and positive morale are essential for sustained success.

The word, inspire means 'breathing in,' which is an activity that is natural, necessary, and ongoing for the healthy living of every human being. Similarly, for any unit that you serve as the leader to remain healthy and vibrant, it must be inspired i.e. it must breathe in life-giving vision, positivity, and a sense of mission regularly, naturally, and as a matter of necessity.

This kind of inspiration is not the product of occasional ceremonies or vision-casting away-days that some organisational leaders use to try and rouse their near comatose workforce. Rather, it is a philosophy of leadership that is woven into the daily fabric of the activities of the unit you lead.

Within a business, inspiration is communicated through recruitment, evaluation, promotion, and other management policies, which communicate that you genuinely care about your workforce. It is communicated daily by letting your team know that what they do is important and serves a noble purpose. It is signalled by letting your staff understand that you care about what happens in their family life as much as what happens in the office. It is letting your people know regularly that they are intrinsically worthy and you sincerely value their contributions to the achievement of your goals and vision.

Extrapolating this into your home (thinking about your work/life balance here…☺), it is a father communicating his love for his children and his belief in their capacity for greatness, on a daily basis. It is a mother actively showing to her family that she values their contributions to the home, however little or big. It is children regularly demonstrating their affection for their parents and valuing their efforts to provide as good a quality of life as they are capable of.

Providing inspiration is the responsibility of leaders at all levels within their arena of influence. In essence, a commitment to leadership means that you are required to be the chief inspiration officer.

3. Personal motivation

One of the quickest ways I have found for identifying leaders is to determine whether they are internally motivated or externally driven. Let me give you an example of what I mean.

Two senior executives of an organisation attended the same training course; when I asked them privately why they were at the course and what they hoped to gain out of it, one responded that it was simply to fulfil his organisation's continuous personal development (CPD) requirements and he would rather be elsewhere, whilst the other responded that although he already had some knowledge and skills in the subject matter covered in the course, he wanted to expand his knowledge and refresh his skills so that he could become a better manager and leader of his department.

As you can tell, these responses are quite revealing. The first executive was 'driven' by an external force (his organisation) and appeared to resent it, whilst the second was internally motivated and relished the opportunity for personal growth that the course presented. It is most likely that either consciously or otherwise, each of these executives would be communicating their attitude towards learning and development to their teams, which would in turn influence how their teams respond to similar opportunities.

So, let me ask you, "Why are you doing whatever you do?" Is it a reflection of your internal motivation as a leader or are you being externally driven by threats and consequences imposed by external parties?

By the way, you may have noticed that I am talking more about the disposition and attitude, rather than the actions by themselves. For example, if past errors happen to have landed you in prison, you may be mandated to maintain a specific routine imposed by the prison authorities, but your internal motivation would be such that you leverage the routine towards achieving positive outcomes for yourself. Some prison inmates have taken the opportunity of such routines to study, obtain university qualifications, and develop their personal capabilities. They simply transmuted what began as external demands into personal internal motivation.

Your journey of leadership will require you to undertake this transmutation process, time and again, because you recognise that one of the hallmarks of effective leaders is their acceptance of the responsibility for personal performance management.

4. Personal productivity

Leaders are judged by results. These results come from a combination of personal and corporate effort. Perhaps I should say the results ought to come from personal **and** corporate effort. This emphasis is required to help tackle the rising phenomenon of lazy leaders who use delegation as an excuse to fob off all their work on their team members. Like me, you've probably heard the heartfelt cry of many an employee who is the victim of irresponsible delegation and is now drowning in a sea of work, whilst the manager lazes about pretending to be busy and important.

Whenever you meet anyone in a position of authority who displays such laziness or irresponsible delegation, it is safe to say that you are meeting a symbol of low-quality leadership.

True leaders are dynamos of personal productivity who have cultivated the principle that they would not demand of their team members more than they demand of themselves. They demonstrate a sense of responsibility through choosing to lead by example, always seeking to contribute the best they are capable of at all times. Does this describe you or those you are leading?

Another phenomenon that is becoming prevalent, at least in the technologically developed, western economies and even more so, in developing countries, is that it is possible to be engaged in frantic activity, day after day, month after month and at the end of a year, have little or nothing to show for it. This is usually the product of a failure to discern the difference between activity and productivity, often reflected in the simple yet profound observation by many researchers that probably up to 95% of people do not have a set of documented personal goals or objectives that they are aiming for.

Goals are a crucial tool for driving your personal productivity. Goals that are properly defined enable you to evaluate whether your activities are taking you towards the achievement of your preferred results or whether you are simply engaged, like a little child, riding a rocking horse frantically but going nowhere. As Bill Walsh, one of the world's foremost business experts teaches, "If you live a goal-oriented life, you achieve more success."

There are many good books that teach the subject of how to set and reach goals effectively. I would encourage you to study this important subject and accept the responsibility for personal productivity by developing a range of goals that serve as milestones on your journey to success.

5. What happens in your absence?

One true measure of a leader's effectiveness is the productivity they inspire in those they lead. But wait just one minute… I am talking here about the productivity you inspire in your absence!

Have you ever heard someone make this statement? "If you want something done right, do it yourself." Or this one, "You just can't get the staff these days." I used to make these statements or variants thereof, many, many years ago until I awoke to the realisation that it was an admission of my poor quality leadership at that time.

The problem was not the staff or the team members. The real problem was that I had not learned how to recruit and develop my team members so that they became and remained effective even in my absence. Simply put, I was cultivating followers instead of raising leaders who were internally motivated to deliver results, especially when I was not in the vicinity to monitor their performance directly.

In my observations of many organisations and ensuing discussions with their leaders, the greatest challenge they have is that productivity plummets in their absence. Why? Because they have not learned how to infuse their teams with the key elements that generate productivity in their absence. These include:

a) **Develop and articulate a clear, compelling vision for your team** – Just like you, those you lead want to know that what they are investing their lives in really matters. They desire that each day of their lives spent with you, is not a fruitless endeavour or an exercise in futility; that what they do with or for you, really does make a positive difference in some way. It is your responsibility as a leader to capture what that positive vision is, and have a mechanism for sharing it actively with your team. This will serve as an anchor of inspiration that will keep them from drifting into unproductive activity when you are away, because they come to understand that their contributions go beyond simply trying to impress you.

b) **Provide measurable goals that track progress towards the fulfilment of the vision** – When people have a specific destination they are aiming for, it is generally easier for them to keep moving even when you are away. Measurable goals that are properly put in place identify whether progress is being made, irrespective of your presence.

c) **Find out what motivates each member of your team** – Every human is motivated by some measure of self-interest. How we choose to describe our motivation will of course vary and whether we admit it or not, at some point we all ask the question, "What's in this for me?"

If the answer you get back from the question is, "not much" or worse still, "nothing", it is just a matter of time before frustration sets in and you begin to plan your exit.

To reduce or avoid a mismatch between the vision and goals you want to accomplish and the internal motivations of your team members, it is crucial to understand that each member of your team asks himself or herself the same question and you need to discover what really motivates them.

I must admit that I chuckle to myself when I hear of organisations that send out questionnaires to their staff members to solicit information on what motivates them. My thought always is, "Are you kidding me?" most of the answers you get back from such questionnaires merely reveal what the staff members require to keep them from walking out of the door in the nearest future.

In order to get to the real kernel of motivation that will drive superlative performance, especially in your absence, you will have to spend quality time with your team members, probing, listening, and observing, and all with a sincere desire to help them achieve their 'dream' as part of the rewards of joining your team.

d) **Align/integrate your team members' goals with your vision** – When you find a way to align the personal goals or motivations of a team member with your own vision, you never have to worry whether they will perform in your absence or not. That is one of the open secrets that have driven the success of the multi-level marketing (MLM) industry. They have found a way to help people rekindle their dreams and integrate these dreams with the achievement of specific levels within the marketing plan of the MLM companies.

Learn how to do the same and you will enjoy a less stressful, enhanced leadership whereby your team deliver great results even in your absence.

e) **Evaluate performance in terms of the integrated goals** – As part of my work over the years, I have had the responsibility for managing teams and often found that annual appraisal time tends to be one of the most daunting periods for many managers and their staff.

For others however, they found it quite enjoyable because they had learned how to evaluate performance, not just with reference to the organisation's goals but with a broader perspective that incorporated the personal dreams and goals of their team members.

The leaders who took an integrated approach found that such an approach made the evaluation process more of honest self-evaluation by the team member, than an imposition of the manager's opinion on how well or poorly the team member had performed.

6. Develop the personal and corporate 'Code of Honour'

A very important responsibility for any leader is to develop the right code of honour for their personal life and the community of people they lead, whether it's a small unit or a large conglomerate. A code of honour can be defined as a set of rules or principles governing a group of people that defines what constitutes honourable behaviour.

The code captures the values, attitudes, and operating philosophy of the leaders of any organisation. The power of the code is that it serves as the foundation of the culture of the community and influences team members' behaviour in many ways, often unconsciously.

The challenge of the code however, is that it rests primarily on one truth, people 'do what you do, not what you say.' That is why so many organisations fail on the integrity issue. If you read through their documented policies, you would probably find reams of papers that demand honest, ethical, decent behaviour from their staff. These unfortunately are not matched by the behaviours the leaders demonstrate to the staff in their daily interactions, therefore the staff members ignore the hypocritical pronouncements in the policy documents and follow the examples of their leaders.

Let me give you a simple example... I meet many people who were once active members of a Christian church, but who left and have become agnostics, atheists, or somehow profoundly disillusioned with matters of faith and religion. When you probe beneath the surface of their angst, you often arrive at a simple, yet widespread problem... the leaders they met in those churches broke the ultimate code of honour for the church... they broke the code of love and their followers did likewise. This then impacted adversely on the people who had to bear the brunt of the lack of love.

So, anyone who desires to be an effective leader is required to establish two crucial practices:

a) **Model the right values... consistently** – In many countries, legislation is often required to force companies to behave properly. Why? Because the leaders repeatedly display appalling behaviour and model the wrong values to their organisation and beyond. This leads to a breakdown of trust between the organisation and its stakeholders.

In many other situations where legislation is not imposed, the behaviour of the leaders also leads to a breakdown of trust between the leader and his followers or the organisation and its stakeholders.

If you say honesty is important, be demonstrably honest. If you say meritocracy is important, don't promote your brother to a position simply because he is your brother, when there are more suitably qualified people to fill the role. If you say transparency is your watchword and you go to great extents to expose what is happening with other people, then you must be transparent, and allow your life and conduct to be examinable by others.

When you model the right values as a leader, you send a clear message to your stakeholders that you are trustworthy.

Let me hasten to add here that I am not advocating that you be a perfect specimen of sainthood all the time. I am saying that if you fall short of the required standards of your code of honour, be humble enough to acknowledge it, apologise for your shortcoming and raise the bar on your level of behaviour.

b) **Enforce the code** – As much as you are responsible for modelling the code of honour, you are also responsible for enforcing it amongst your team.

This demands a sense of justice and fair play. Equal infringements of the code must receive equal sanction. No exceptions. And equal demonstrations of laudable conduct must receive equal commendation.

Have you experienced a situation where two people committed the same offence yet the leader allowed one person to get off lightly whilst the other was severely penalised? You instinctively know something is wrong with such a situation. You may not be in a position to say something about it but in your estimation, that leader lost some measure of credibility.

When you ignore or belittle infringements of the code of honour, you send a signal to others that you do not value the code, and if you do not value the code, why should anyone else?

Consistently modelling and reinforcing the code of honour in words and actions will set you apart as a leader worth following.

1. Succession

One of the most important responsibilities a leader can embrace is to hand over the baton of leadership successfully to the next leader, who has been properly prepared to take the organisation to a higher level of success. This is the principle of succession planning.

You have probably heard the stories of pioneers, who built their enterprises, but because of poor succession planning, when they passed away or handed over the reins of leadership, the enterprise nosedived and what they had built over years or decades, crumbled rapidly.

Sometimes, when I undertook an interim management project, one of the statements I made to the team when I joined them was this; "I came to leave… and over the next few months, I aim to find my replacement among you." This was often a shock to them as they were used to managers who were more interested in keeping them down than raising them up.

This principle of proper succession is captured in these words, "Leaders know that if their vision dies with them, they have failed. The ultimate goal is not to maintain followers but to produce leaders."[3]

As you build your home, business, organisation, or enterprise of any kind, cultivate an attitude that envisions your enterprise outliving you and continuing to grow without you. With this in mind, let us consider some of the ways in which you can accomplish this.

a) Have the right systems in place

In this context, a system is a structured way of undertaking an activity that can be documented and transferred to others to perform.

Having the right systems in place enables your organisation to have a modus operandi that is independent of the actual individuals carrying out the activity. I once heard this idea humorously described as, 'no one monkey must stop the show'.

Systems help to depersonalise the daily routines required to keep your enterprise thriving in your absence. This means that other people will be able to step in and keep things going when the original owner of a task or activity is unavailable and that includes the leader.

Develop your systems in the key areas of your enterprise activity and train your team members to use the systems. If the systems are not working as well as hoped, there is a tendency for people to abandon the systems and set up their own way of doing things. The problem is that their approach may not be transferable and when they leave, their area of activity and the organisation suffers.

Therefore, if the systems are not working, refine them or replace them... but ensure you do have a system in place. This is one of the primary ways to ensure that your vision outlasts you.

b) Coach for success

Identify potential leaders and take the time to coach them into becoming the kind of leader that can propel your enterprise into a greater future. This requires a solid investment of time, effort, and patience as you infuse the upcoming leaders with your values, wisdom, opportunities for growth, and your credibility.

So, if you have a successful enterprise right now, let me ask you three questions:

1. If you suddenly became incapacitated today, what would happen to your enterprise? Would it keep growing without you or stagnate?

2. Who has been prepared to take over and is capable of taking your enterprise to greater heights of success?

3. What are you doing to mentor and coach them into successful leadership?

If your enterprise is in a fledgling state, congratulations, you now have three core questions to keep in mind as you recruit new team members to join in building your enterprise.

I would encourage you to embrace the diversity of responsibilities outlined in this section, as they can serve you greatly in your pursuit to become a more effective leader in your arena of influence.

Responsibility – Interactive Exercise

In what areas have you demonstrated a great sense of responsibility?

_____

_____

_____

In what areas have you NOT demonstrated the right sense of leadership responsibility? (And why not?)

_____

_____

_____

What will you do to take responsibility where required? (And when?)

_____

_____

_____

Do you practice responsible delegation? (If YES, describe how. Are there areas to improve upon? How will you improve upon them?)

_____

_____

_____

Are you the Chief Inspiration Officer within your sphere of influence? (If YES, describe how you do it. If NO; how can you help to inspire others within your sphere?)

_____

_____

_____

Are you a dynamo of personal productivity? (If YES, describe how. If NO; how can you improve your productivity?)

_____

_____

_____

Are you externally driven or internally motivated? (And why? What keeps you the way you are?)

_____

_____

_____

What happens to the productivity of your team in your absence? (And why?)

_____

_____

_____

What will you do to INSPIRE increased productivity within your team?

_____

_____

_____

Who are you preparing to receive the baton of leadership from you? (Name them)

_____

_____

_____

What specifically are you doing to prepare your protégés for effective leadership?
(What activities and how frequently?)

_____

_____

_____

What other questions arise for you from this section?

_____

_____

_____

What will you do in response to these additional questions?

_____

_____

_____

Integrity

At the core of the leadership jigsaw is integrity. It is the rock solid foundation upon which quality, long lasting leadership can be built.

A leader can make mistakes for a whole plethora of reasons. As a business leader, you may have been given incorrect or insufficient information to facilitate the right decision. Or as a political leader, you may have misjudged the potential impact of your decisions on some stakeholders. As a mother, you might have done what you thought was best for your child based on the available facts, only to realise later that you were wrong.

People are often willing to forgive these kinds of mistakes, because we all understand that no human is perfect. However, if a review of your actions or decisions indicates that the problem was a matter of integrity, the repercussions to your leadership are far more damaging.

The many lapses of the former president of the U.S.A, Bill Clinton are well documented for posterity. Despite his misguided illicit liaison with Monica Lewinsky, the American electorate were not overly concerned. When he compounded his poor judgement by lying about the relationship, his entire political career almost unravelled and he threw the office of president and his nation into a tremendous political crisis as the nation reacted to his lack of integrity.

Despite his overarching power in the politics of Italy, former Prime Minister Silvia Berlusconi's greatest challenge often comes from the perceptions and accusations of corruption and a lack of integrity.

In the United Kingdom, the parliamentary body was thrown into disrepute when the scandal of members of parliament (MP) expenses was revealed. The political careers of some MPs were prematurely terminated as a result and the electorate grew even more disillusioned with the leadership of the nation.

Many other examples abound of the destructive effects of a lack of integrity. The global climate change movement has taken a severe battering, because of the lack of integrity demonstrated by some academics in a British university.

Latin American and African nations are repeatedly castigated because of the lack of integrity prevalent amongst many of the so-called leaders in those nations. As an example, before he passed away, over 170 million Nigerians were left bewildered by a situation where the president of the nation, Umaru Yar' Adua was incommunicado for over eighty days due to ill health. The political leadership continuously released a poisonous mix of half-truths and pure fabrications about the state of his health, which plunged the nation into a state of crisis and fears of a military coup.

Corruption, bribery, social injustice, rampant electoral malpractices etc. are the order of the day in many of the underdeveloped, Third World countries, and this filters through into the low level of social, educational, and political development in these nations. There is a very high cost attached to a lack of integrity.

Religious institutions are just as tainted by the lack of integrity as secular institutions. The Catholic Church is paying out billions of dollars in many parts of the world as compensation to the victims of sexual abuse by catholic priests.

All of these are high profile incidences recorded in the news media, but the need for integrity is not limited to high profile leaders. I contend that everyone is a leader in some arena of life and we all need to walk in integrity.

Why – because integrity is the cornerstone of trust and respect. Simple acts of a lack of integrity in your daily life may not be splashed on the front pages of a newspaper, but they are written on the tabloids of the minds of those who are watching you.

As a management consultant, I have undertaken projects with major organisations in the UK and this affords me the opportunity to test my leadership ideas and also observe the various expressions of leadership capability in these different environments.

I remember a project where I participated in my first meeting with the staff members of a local authority department. After listening to the team for about an hour, it was evident that the fundamental problem with the department was the exceptionally poor quality of leadership the department had experienced. And the source of their greatest irritation was their perception of the lack of integrity of their previous manager.

Due to this perception, instructions and decisions had to be confirmed in triplicates of emails because according to them, "You simply couldn't trust what management says." This scenario is played out in possibly thousands of organisations around the world where paper and electronic documentation proliferates, not just to maintain proper records, but as it is colloquially put, to 'cover your backside.' Trust has broken down within these organisations and this exacts a very heavy cost in wasted time, effort, and resources.

The names Enron, Lehman Brothers, Rio Tinto in China, and Halliburton in America all conjure up images of broken trust and tarnished integrity. Indeed, there are many who argue that the 2008 global financial meltdown is a result of the fundamental lack of integrity and poor character that characterised the major players in the banking sector and even financial regulators.

So the question is this…

What about you? How do you stack up in the integrity index?

First, let us define integrity. *Dictionary.com* defines integrity as 'adherence to moral and ethical principles; soundness of moral character; honesty.' It also defines it as 'the state of being whole, entire or undiminished.'

I would add that integrity is the proper alignment of noble moral values in the right order of priority. When a strongly held, personal moral principle collides with another, the tension has to be resolved by understanding the right priority level of each principle and realigning them correctly.

To demonstrate this tension, consider an executive of a company that is having some major financial difficulty and if the company does not win its next contract it will have to go into bankruptcy; he is committed to pursuing the financial success of his company so that his economic future and the livelihoods of the company's employees and their families are not threatened... this is a noble sentiment.

However, in his bid to win the major contract he encounters a client representative who demands a bribe to facilitate the success of his bid. This executive's value orientation of honesty is now on a collision path with the values of protecting the interests of those in his care... what does he choose?

Both sets of values are individually noble, the question is, "In what order of priority does he hold those values?" How would you resolve this tension?

This is where another definition of integrity becomes worthy of our consideration – Integrity is the convergence of a person's private and public persona. In essence, if who you are in private is not the same as who you are in public, there is a lack of integrity.

This is where transparency as a core leadership principle holds sway. To return to our previous example above, offering the bribe would necessarily be a private transaction, but when the light of public scrutiny is shed on this private event, it takes on a different hue called corruption. So transparency serves as the umpire in resolving the tension between the different values this business executive holds.

Similarly, your personal integrity is reinforced by your commitment to transparency.

As an effective leader, integrity is not just a personal issue; it is always a public matter, because integrity is the interface between you and everyone else with whom you interact. The first question at the back of the mind of everyone who meets you is, "Can I trust you?" And they assess their further association with you on the basis of how this question is answered by your words and actions.

In their book, *The Leadership Challenge*, James Kouzes & Barry Posner revealed the results of surveys they conducted for more than fifteen years to over 75,000 respondents on all continents around the globe. They said, "In almost every survey we've conducted, honesty has been selected more often than any other leadership characteristic; overall it emerges as the single most important ingredient in the leader-constituent relationship." [44]

The importance of your integrity as a leader simply cannot be overemphasised; it is the bedrock of personal and corporate success.

In the words of Oren Harari, "A lack of integrity is not simply an ethical concern; it also poses a clear threat to the effective functioning of the organization." [5]

This perspective is borne out by a survey undertaken by *Sales and Marketing* magazine in February 2001. Among those surveyed, they found that:

❖ 58% cheat on expense reports

❖ 50% work a second job on company time

❖ 36% rush closed deals through accounting, before they were really closed

❖ 22% list a "strip bar" as a restaurant on an expense report

❖ 19% give a kickback to a customer

In the 2009 National Business Ethics Survey conducted by the Ethics Research Centre, the survey reported the following:

❖ People who had witnessed ethical misconduct on the job – 49%

❖ People that had reported misconduct when they observed it – 63%

❖ The strength of ethical culture in the workplace – 62%

Some of their conclusions include that, "Principles of transparency and accountability are integral to ethical culture." One of the components of ethical culture is Ethical leadership in which leaders set the right 'tone at the top' and model ethical culture as part of earning the trust of employees.

This is reinforced by the Deloitte & Touche USA 2007 Ethics & Workplace survey that stated, "Specifically, when asked to identify the top factors for promoting an ethical workplace, 77% of working adults cite either the behaviour of management, or of direct supervisors, as setting the tone for ethical behaviour." Every leader would do well to heed General Colin Powell's advice that, "Whatever the cost, do what is right."

So let me ask this question again, how do you stack up in the personal integrity index? What are the areas of improvement that you need to work on?

And how do you model integrity to your family, employees, pupils, friends, business associates, or other stakeholders, depending on what arena of life you operate in?

This brings us to the idea that integrity is evaluated by the congruence of your thoughts, words, and actions. When there is a lack of congruence between these three elements of your life, it manifests itself in hypocrisy. Integrity is about being authentic as a person and as a leader. It is about being yourself… the real you.

The highly respected business guru, Warren Bennis agrees that, "Becoming a leader is synonymous with becoming yourself. It's that simple and that difficult." [6]

Tools and methods for developing effective leadership can never take the place of the authentic you. Applying leadership skills that are incongruent with your true self will reveal itself quickly in inconsistencies that strip you of credibility and diminish your leadership influence.

So the quest for high quality leadership is inevitably a quest in personal authenticity and integrity and therefore a commitment to the ongoing journey of self-discovery.

How do you recover from integrity failure?

Failure in some form or the other is an experience that every leader has had to contend with. As Albert Einstein once said, "If you have never made a mistake, you have never tried anything new."

Of all leadership crises however, the most difficult to recover from is the crisis of integrity failure, because these types of failure threaten the very foundation of any leadership structure… the relationship of trust between the leader and his stakeholders.

The outgoing President of China and General Secretary of the Chinese Communist Party in his opening speech to the delegates of the party's

18ᵗʰ National Congress in November 2012 highlighted the critical nature of the issue of integrity. He told them, and by extension, the over 1.2 billion citizens of China, that corruption and lack of integrity, "could prove fatal to the party, and even cause the collapse of the party and the fall of the state."

Having said this, it is also important to understand that even failures of integrity do not have to be terminal… You can recover from them and rise to new heights.

An instructive example of how to recover from such failure comes from the experiences of President Clinton whom as I mentioned earlier, threw his nation into crisis over a personal relationship. His recovery can be traced to some key steps that anyone can emulate as a pathway to recovery from a lapse of integrity.

a) Apologise sincerely – without excuses

Attempting to excuse his behaviour would have been even more inflammatory to his family, friends, and nation and would have nullified any potential positive benefit from his apology.

You've probably heard the kind of apology that sounds something like, "I am sorry, but…" (you can fill in the space with whatever excuse was given). How did you feel when someone offered you such an apology? Probably made you feel even more offended, didn't it? Such an apology reveals that the person offering it is passing the blame and is not really sincere.

President Clinton avoided such a costly mistake. He did not offer such a hollow apology. He apologised sincerely, without excuses, to his family, friends, and nation and he took full responsibility for his actions.

And his family and nation forgave him.

b) Allow people to heal

It takes time for people to heal from the distress caused by a lapse of integrity, so allow your constituents the time and space necessary to go through the emotional process from hurt to healing to fully healed.

Don't demand loyalty or commitment from people who are hurting from your actions or words that already represent a betrayal of trust for them. As intuitive as this may sound, I am still amazed at how many leaders ignore this basic principle and expect things to continue as normal when their constituents are still reeling from the impact of their lack of integrity, no matter how small or big.

If you need to take a leave of absence, do so. If a temporary transfer of a position of authority is required, do it graciously.

If you ignore this process of allowing people to heal, most of your constituents will terminate their emotional contract with you, even if they show up to work the next day. From then on, all you have are the bodies of the people; you no longer have their heart, passion, and commitment to your vision. In essence, your true leadership with them is dead.

c) Rebuild trust on a daily basis

True leadership is a daily exchange of trust between leaders and followers. Commit to rebuilding trust with your stakeholders by your daily actions and words that demonstrate integrity, sound character, and the right moral values, which underpin your healthy relationship with them, and which remind them of why they subscribed to your leadership in the first place.

d) Do not become a hostage to the past

As awful as it sounds, there are some people who would like to see you fail and would want you and others to wallow continually in the cesspit of the memories of your past failures. These kinds of people would always seek to bring up your past, despite your best efforts to demonstrate a sincere transformation and renewed commitment to integrity.

Never allow such people to make you a hostage to your past. And even more critically, as a leader, never allow your own thinking to mire you in the past failure.

President Clinton rebuilt his leadership influence and he continues to impact our world positively, through his work with the Clinton Global Foundation.

You have made a genuine commitment to living a present and future life of integrity; now get on with it! The world awaits the benefits of all the greatness that still lies within you.

Integrity – Interactive Exercise

On a scale of 1 to 10 (1 = lowest; 10 = highest), what is your score on the personal integrity index? (Is this the best you can be? What area needs improvement?)

_____

_____

_____

On a scale of 1 to 10 (1 = lowest; 10 = highest), what is the level of integrity prevalent in your arena of influence? (e.g. workplace, home, or other key area of life for you.)

_____

_____

_____

What are the three main reasons responsible for this level of integrity in your chosen arena (s)?

_____

_____

_____

What will you do to INSPIRE an increase in the level of integrity in your arena (s) of influence?

_____

_____

_____

What other questions arise for you from this section?

_____

_____

_____

What will you do in response to these additional questions?

_____

_____

_____

Personal Growth

All effective leaders possess an unyielding dedication to continuous personal growth. They recognise that knowledge becomes obsolete very fast in the rapidly changing, hypercompetitive environment of the 21st century.

They understand the truth captured by John F. Kennedy's words, "Leadership and learning are indispensable to each other." [7]

There are several modes of learning, which serve different people in different ways. As a leader, it is useful to explore the different approaches available and determine which best maximises your personal capabilities and preferences.

These learning modes are captured in the diagram below, which is based on the famous cone of experience developed by Edgar Dale, an American professor of Education at Ohio University.

The cone indicates that generally, the level of effective learning and retention increases when the learning activity incorporates more aspects of our physical senses. So, people generally retain about 10% of what they have read after approximately two weeks, about 50% of what they see and hear (e.g. watching a demonstration or attending an exhibition) whilst they retain approximately 90% when the learning experience utilises almost all senses of touch, sight, smell, hearing etc. such that it approximates closely to the real thing (e.g. simulations or presentations).

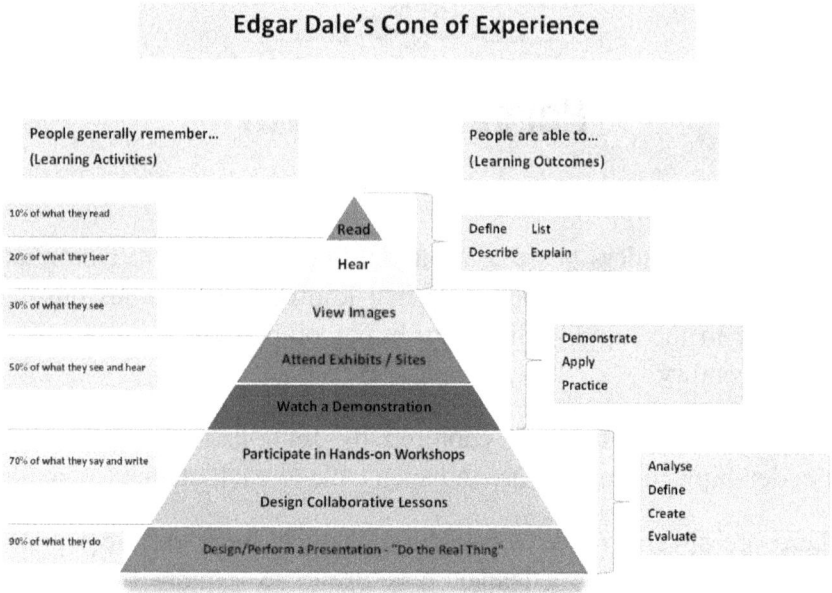

Dale's Cone of Experience (Construct) – Image courtesy of Dr R.S Pastore (2013)[8]

There is some debate amongst academics about the relative percentages of material retained after two weeks. However, the overarching message here is for you to consider using the different styles, modes, and avenues of learning, particularly those that engage all your senses actively i.e. hearing, sight, touch etc. Many educational experts affirm that learning experiences that incorporate as many of our senses as possible are usually more effective in aiding the acquisition and retention of knowledge; this is called accelerated learning.

This accords with the principle that true learning is not just cerebral i.e. just taking in knowledge mentally, it is also experiential i.e. lived out. Knowledge truly becomes yours when you have incorporated it into your personal experience and mindset.

There is a direct correlation between your personal development and your success in any area of life. As Dr Mike Murdock aptly puts it, "Every problem in life is a wisdom problem." Or put another way, something you don't know may be destroying you.

Therefore, the continuous journey of personal growth is not simply a good idea; it is a critical necessity. And not only is it critical for you, it is critical for any organisation or enterprise that you lead.

You are likely familiar with the principle that a chain is only as strong as its weakest link or that a convoy travels as fast as its slowest vehicle. This is true for your team as well.

Hence, if you desire for your organisation to grow, thrive, or even survive in this age of rapid and often explosive change, not only should you be committed to personal development, you must insist on it from those who expect to remain part of your team. If not, those who remain trapped in yesterday's knowledge will become the Achilles heel of your organisation, a source of weakness that can eventually lead to destruction.

However, not only must you insist on personal development from your team members, you must actively facilitate it, either through signposting them to requisite resources or better still, make the tools and resources available to them. Great leadership infuses an organisation with the spirit of learning and innovation.

One of the requirements for effective leadership is the capacity to solve problems and as Albert Einstein once quipped, "We can't solve problems by using the same kind of thinking we used when we created them." Suffice it to say that your level of quality thinking only grows through active personal development.

Align with personal purpose

Many people who are interested in personal development often pursue it in a haphazard manner, studying books, audiovisual material, attending workshops, or seminars in no coherent manner whatsoever.

The challenge is that there is so much information available that it can become overwhelming... And it is increasing exponentially. According to latest estimates, knowledge available to us is doubling virtually every two years and the computer giant, IBM, anticipates that soon, this doubling of available knowledge will happen every eleven hours.

That's right... eleven hours to render much of your past knowledge obsolete.

So how do we cope with this vast amount of information? By focussing even more closely on what is important. And I would add that the definition of what is important is, "the degree to which the information is necessary for the achievement of your personal purpose or mission in life."

Measure your activity

It is virtually impossible to evaluate properly an activity you don't measure. So in order to get a good sense of whether you are heading up or down in your personal development, measure your personal training.

- ❖ How many books did you read in the last six months that are related to your vision?

- ❖ How many audio-visual materials did you study?

- ❖ How many hours did you spend communicating with a mentor?

- ❖ How many seminars, workshops, conferences, or other experiential learning events did you attend?

If you are unaware of how much time and effort you are putting into these activities, it is unlikely that you will be able to evaluate objectively their effectiveness in contributing to your growth.

Most organisations that send their staff on training courses often require their staff and departments to keep a log of all the training activities they have attended in the year. This helps with evaluating value for money of those courses they have spent their resources on. I believe that as a leader, you should also keep a personal log of all training activities you undertake, whether within or outside your formal working environment.

This will serve as a tool for evaluating the direction in which you are travelling in respect of your personal growth.

Evaluate and refine

As mentioned earlier, the world around us is changing at a dizzying pace, so it is important to evaluate whether the developmental activities you have undertaken are fulfilling the following objectives:

❖ Does the training keep you at the cutting edge of current developments in your chosen industry?

  If you always have to find out from colleagues at work about legislative, technological, political, or other changes affecting your industry, something is wrong.

❖ Has the training equipped you with a specific competence or skill that you have personally identified as necessary for consolidating success at the current level?

❖ What proportion of your training activities is equipping you for your next level of personal leadership?

❖ Most importantly, are these activities properly aligned to your personal purpose?

With your objective evaluation complete, set new goals for your development. You may need to seek out new sources of learning, new mentors or study at a more advanced level. Remember, as a leader, growth is never-ending.

One thing that is absolutely critical to emphasize is this, particularly if you are currently working as an employee within an organisation; personal development must become a philosophy of life, not just a mechanical compliance with organisational requirements.

Until you take joy in the principle and practice of self-development, any training opportunities offered to you will seem like an imposition by your supervisor or manager, just so that you can have something to show during your annual appraisal. That is the mindset of mediocrity, not that of a leader.

As a leader, you joyfully accept the responsibility for your own growth within your organisation and help steer the training offered in the direction that will create win-win outcomes for you and your company.

The commitment to personal development is another piece in the jigsaw. The more you grow, the more your leadership influence expands. Incorporate this piece in your life and you raise the level of your leadership effectiveness.

Apply funnel vision

I recently spoke to a young friend and asked him what book he had bought in the last three months. His response was, "I never buy a book." When I asked why, he responded that he felt that the internet provided him with all the information he needed. I had to laugh at his naivety because he had unwittingly discounted one of the most powerful sources of information still available to us today. As useful as internet search engines are, it would be foolhardy to rely totally on that one avenue of information, which is a collation of disparate, often contradictory, unstructured material.

That said… there is a plethora of information available for you online on virtually any subject whatsoever. Type the subject into the Google search engine and you would most likely have tens of thousands, if not millions of 'hits' or references to that subject.

Whilst you need to be very discerning and ensure that your pursuit of knowledge is aligned with your purpose, be alert to the possibility that you may be obtaining your information from too narrow a source, which can prejudice the quality of your insights. Develop a funnel vision that continually explores an ever-increasing source of quality information, which helps you remain on the cutting edge of your leadership capabilities.

For example, the subject of leadership shows up in many areas such as science, business, politics, religion, education, sports etc., so if you are a school teacher, you would find it helpful to look beyond the field of academic education and stretch your funnel to tap into ideas available from the other areas of endeavour such as sports and business in order to expand your knowledge on leadership.

Invest in yourself

Let me ask you these questions:

- ❖ What is the highest amount you have ever <u>personally</u> paid for a book, CD, DVD, seminar or other programme that serves the express purpose of self-development?

- ❖ In the last 12 months, have you spent more on food, clothing, accessories for your body than on nourishment for your mind?

- ❖ What do your responses to the last two questions tell you about your commitment to developing yourself and your leadership capabilities?

Now, consider the five people that you spend most of your time with and ask the same question about them. Whether you like it or not, these five people are the thermometer of your success. When we study them and their willingness to invest in their personal growth, we have a clear measure of whom you are or who you are becoming. We can tell whether you are experiencing the raging 'fever' of growth and success or the hypothermia of mediocrity and failure.

High-quality learning and development is not cheap… But neither are you!

So, be willing to invest the necessary resources required, to chisel the latent abilities within you into sparkling gems of leadership greatness.

Personal Growth – Interactive Exercise

What is the highest amount you have ever <u>personally</u> paid for a personal growth resource? (e.g. a book, CD, DVD, seminar etc.)

_____

_____

_____

What activities did you undertake for personal growth in the last three months? (List them here and how frequently e.g. read one book per week or attended one seminar per month.)

_____

_____

_____

Are the activities aligned with your personal purpose? (State how.)

_____

_____

_____

What new skill, ability, innovative idea, or other capability have you developed as a result of the personal growth activities?

_____

_____

_____

What do your responses to these 'growth questions' reveal about your commitment to developing your personal leadership?

_____

_____

_____

What about the team you lead. Would their responses to these 'growth questions', reveal a commitment to personal and team growth or not? (And what will you do about it?)

_____

_____

_____

What other questions arise for you from this section?

_____

_____

_____

What will you do in response to these additional questions?

_____

_____

_____

Strategic Competences

There are distinctions between the person (i.e. being the leader – internal mastery) and the practices (i.e. doing the leadership function – external influence) when we discuss leadership as a human experience.

There is an intricate overlap between these two, but they are definitely distinct, which I think is why many institutions, including management schools, fail to develop quality leaders. They often focus on teaching the practices of leadership and relegate the more important aspect of 'being' a leader.

The aim of the Leadership Jigsaw is to provide a balanced approach to these two perspectives, so that you will emerge from our time together as a higher quality leader who not only possesses the heart of a true leader, but who has also developed a robust set of capabilities that equip you for external influence. I describe these capabilities as strategic competencies.

They are strategic in the sense that acquiring them as part of your skill set can be the major determining factor in the long-term success or failure of your endeavour. They encompass the following:

1. Strategic thinking

This is the type of thinking that is supposedly the exclusive preserve of the elite leaders at the top of organisations or businesses. If you have been misled into believing such a notion, let me assure you that it is a false notion that you have to jettison, in order to be the kind of leader that you were born to be.

Strategic thinking simply comprises specific elements, which anyone can apply to their own arenas of life. If you have those components, you are thinking strategically. If you don't have those elements, regardless of where you sit on the totem pole of any organisational structure, the thinking is non-strategic.

So, what are these specific elements?

It is holistic and integrated – This means it is opposite, to the kind of thinking that only takes in a narrow perspective on people, events, or circumstances that affect you or your team. For example, if you are a father with a household for which you are responsible, strategic thinking demands that you go beyond the narrow confines of what you want for yourself, to thinking about what is in the best interests of your entire family. You integrate your personal needs with those of your family to arrive at a composite solution that is best for all.

If you are a head teacher at a school, you factor in the needs of your pupils, your teachers, and other stakeholders as part of your thinking process; you do not make decisions that would merely make you look good with the education board, despite its detrimental effects on all other stakeholders.

It is long range and future oriented – There are always a plethora of decisions that you need to take on a day-to-day basis, most of which do not determine whether your organisation survives into the future or not. Strategic thinking involves the thinking that helps you focus on what you need to do today, so that the long-term future of your enterprise is assured.

Again, taking the simple example of a parent, have you considered saving some money consistently towards the future university education of your children even though they might be in primary school right now? That is long-range thinking and it is important to the future success of your family.

If you are running a business, are your decisions and actions based on the long-term future of the organisation or are they based on trying to make a quick buck in the short term? The former is strategic and the latter is not.

It is realistic – Proper strategic thinking must result in a definitive action plan that can be realistically implemented. If it does not result in demonstrable action, it is wishful thinking, not strategic. If it does not result in an implementable plan, it is muddled thinking, not strategic.

It is flexible – With the best will in the world, there will be situations and circumstances that arise that were totally unforeseeable. It is virtually impossible to 'manage' such situations as part of your original plans. Real strategic thinking maintains a flexibility that is able to respond actively and effectively to emerging scenarios. You maintain a focus on your destination while allowing that a new direction may be required to get you there.

It is synergistic – What I mean is that it is a way of thinking that synthesises information from a broad range of stakeholders and builds on it to generate win-win solutions.

This is one area where humility in the leader is of great value. I have listened to organisational leaders defending a position that favours their own department without any regard for the impact on the overall organisation. For them, success has become a zero-sum game where they only succeed at the expense of others. This is non-synergistic and non-strategic thinking.

The engine that drives this type of quality thinking is simply the type of questions you ask as part of your thinking process. If you focus your questions in a way that is designed to incorporate these five core elements, you will reap the generous benefits of strategic thinking.

Ask questions such as:

- ❖ What is the potential impact of implementing this idea on the long-term future of my business or organisation?

- ❖ How will my actions affect my family overall?

- ❖ What are the benefits of this decision for my community or country? Who benefits or loses? How and why?

- ❖ Am I simply chasing a short-term benefit at the expense of a more rewarding long-term outcome?

- ❖ How will this action position my business to survive and thrive in the light of emerging trends?

Hopefully, you get the general idea. You can enhance your competence in strategic thinking as a tool to raise yourself and your constituents to a new level of accomplishments.

2. The capacity to handle change and crises

Mary Chapman, the former chief executive of the UK Chartered Management Institute once said, "Looking ahead ten years, it is clear that the successful organisations will be those that can do more than embrace change – they will anticipate, identify and drive it."

This organisational capacity for driving change begins with the leader's ability to handle change effectively and since much of the change masquerades as crisis, it serves us well to develop leadership skills for handling crises.

The first line in Rudyard Kipling's celebrated poem titled 'IF' runs thus:

*"IF you can keep your head when all about you are losing theirs and blaming it on yo*u*…"*

And the poem concludes with the line:

"Yours is the Earth and everything that's in it, and - which is more - you'll be a Man, my son!"

These two lines again highlight this requisite strategic competency of an effective leader... the ability to handle crises effectively and remain calm in the midst of them.

This is a competence that can be developed, first by understanding the benefits of crises and then harnessing those benefits as a tool for enhancing your leadership ability. Let us explore this in a little more detail.

In this context, our working definition for a crisis is 'an unplanned and unmanaged change event'; therefore your assessment of any situation as a crisis is a direct expression of your perceived capacity or otherwise, to manage that change event effectively.

Some of the benefits of a crisis include:

Crisis tests your vision – According to business statistics, almost 95% of businesses in the United Kingdom, America, and other developed economies end in failure. In the UK, most of these businesses fail in the first five years. These are the ones that gave up on their vision when the going got tough. When a crisis arose, they threw in the towel.

A crisis is an opportunity to evaluate your commitment to the vision of your family, business, or any other important area of your life. Or it may be the clarion call to develop and refine a long-term vision.

A robust long-term vision enables you to put crises into proper perspective. An effective leader sees a crisis as a temporary anomaly that will yield to his or her 'never-give-up' attitude.

In regard to relationships, crises also reveal the strength of your friendships, business associations, or other connections. True friends are those who emerge with you from the swirling dust of temporary failure, problems, or crises, still committed to you and cheering you on to victory.

Crisis exposes your weaknesses – Good, fortuitous times tend to mask the weaknesses in our lives, businesses, communities, or nations. For example, surges in petroleum oil prices dramatically exposed the strategic weaknesses in the economies of many western nations through their dependence on foreign oil.

Rather than bemoan this dependence as many have done in the past, President Barack Obama turned it into a motivator for American energy independence.

In African nations that are getting excited about oil finds, the recurrent spike in petroleum prices appears to be a bonus, which unfortunately blinds them to a powerful trend, the simple truth that the rest of the world is actively pursuing the goal of rendering this product obsolete through innovative 'green' technologies and other sources of power generation.

As a leader, crisis provides you with an excellent opportunity to appraise your weaknesses objectively, evaluate the emerging trends, and understand your personal resilience and strategic options... Then do something about what you find out.

Crisis opens doors for the deployment of your unique capabilities – You have unique gifts, talents, or abilities, which you may have ignored or which may have been ignored by those around you. For example, in the business arena, you might have creative marketing skills or product development strengths that could generate significant business growth, but which have been lying dormant. However, when a crisis erupts, it often creates the opportunity to shine a bright spotlight on your distinctive capabilities, which had previously been ignored.

Be sensitive to these opportunities and allow your unique qualities to come to the fore. When these opportunities arise, ask yourself key questions such as:

a) What creative approach can I deploy in solving this issue?

b) What solution resides inside of me as the answer to this family, business, community, national, or global question?

Then explore avenues to contribute your creativity and innovation to the resolution of the challenges.

Crisis forces you to confront and refine your paradigms – A wise man once said, "As a man thinks in his heart (i.e. his subconscious mind), so is he." This emphasises that you live according to your assumptions and convictions about life and living effectively... what we call your 'world view.'

Crisis, however, forces you to confront the deficiencies of your thinking. Therefore, as an effective leader, such a confrontation should result in a refinement of your assumptions, leading to a healthy paradigm shift.

For example, the coalition leaders involved in the military intervention in Afghanistan, assumed that toppling the Taliban would bring immediate positive results and create a democratic nation quickly, but the euphoria of the first few months soon wore off as the insurgency began.

The resulting crisis for American and British forces however, forced the leaders to reappraise their assumptions. Consequently, the strategy for dealing with the Afghan question had to be revised and peace talks with the erstwhile enemy came under consideration.

Similarly, what assumptions are you making concerning your business, job, relationships, or other arena of life? Do the results so far support your assumptions? If not, revise your paradigm, make a new set of choices, and then move forward.

From the above, I trust you will understand that crisis is not your enemy. Pain is evidence that new thinking or a new approach is required.

Every crisis reintroduces you to yourself and your core values, and requests a reassessment of your vision and your capabilities. Your mandate is to use these crises and the application of the above principles as part of your development.

This will in turn equip you with a greater sense of confidence, a more refined and durable skill set, and a dynamism that makes you more valuable to your stakeholders, whether in your family, business, or in a national or global context.

3. High level communication skills

You may have heard some person say something like, "leadership is not a popularity contest." This is often stated as a means of justifying why that person is ignoring the complaints and criticisms of those around them.

Well, I beg to differ. Such a notion flies in the face of all known empirical evidence since the dawn of time. Leadership **is** a popularity contest! And one of the most powerful tools of this contest is effective communication.

Evil men and their destructive ideas have flourished, because they have been allowed to take the communication high ground and disseminate their noxious ideas into the minds of people. Nazism, Stalinism and extremist Islamism are cases in point.

On a more personal level, like me, you have probably experienced situations either in the workplace, amongst your friends, or in other endeavours where foolishness has prevailed because wiser minds remained silent.

You are a repository of ideas, answers, and solutions that our world desperately needs and you owe it to humanity to communicate these to us so that our world can be a better place because you showed up.

There are numerous studies on the art of effective communication and there are equally numerous books on the subject, so I won't be tackling this in great depth here. I will trust you as a leader who is committed to personal growth, to seek out the additional resources that will help you complete this bit of your own personal leadership jigsaw. As a start, one of the best books I could recommend is "How to win friends and influence people" by Dale Carnegie.

There are however, some crucial points I want to make about this important subject.

Establish your purpose clearly – In your attempt to communicate with an audience, whether it is one person or a thousand, it is crucial to understand and clearly establish the exact purpose for your interaction. Generally there are three core purposes for communicating with others.

- ❖ To elicit information.

- ❖ To instruct.

- ❖ To inspire.

If you are unclear about the purpose of your communication activity, do not be surprised that your audience is even more confused with the inevitable negative reaction to your efforts.

I made such a mistake many years ago and it was not a happy occasion for me or the audience. What happened was that I had been invited by a medium-sized charity in London to review their administrative operations and produce a report for the senior management team on ways in which they could improve, or so I thought.

The assignment brief came to me through a friend and I neglected to double-check this with the senior management of the charity, when I arrived to commence the project. I spent three days there and produced a report for them; at which point, all hell broke loose.

It became evident that I had failed to establish the clear and proper purpose for the project or my written communication that would emerge from it.

It transpired that the report I had produced was not meant for the senior management team, but was meant to be submitted to the regulatory officials scheduled to visit the charity shortly. Obviously, there were observations I had made in my report that the charity were not overly keen to share with their regulators at that time.

I have also been a part of seminar or conference audiences on the receiving end of speakers, who were completely clueless on the purpose of their communication activity. They rambled on and on, neither instructing, nor inspiring the audience and ended up wasting both their time and ours.

Whenever you want to communicate via speaking or writing, I urge you to develop crystal clarity about the purpose your communication is meant to achieve, and structure your activity to deliver this as simply as possible.

Know the purpose of your audience – You simply cannot assume what they need or want from you. Hopefully, my examples above make this point clearly.

Some time ago, I undertook a project for a public sector organisation in the UK that involved the production of a report that would shape a major government policy initiative. I found that one of the most difficult areas of that project for me was trying to understand the expectations of the audience for whom I was writing. If I got this wrong, the report would most likely end up on the scrap heap and my reputation would take a severe battering.

I had learned my lesson from previous experiences, one of which I have described above. In order to compensate for this potential weakness therefore, I ensured that I received input from as many sources as possible to help me understand whom I was targeting with the report. I am pleased to say that my efforts to know my audience paid off in highly complementary feedback on the report, from some of the most important stakeholders in the project.

Adapt your methods – Particularly when communicating with individuals, customisation is king. There is an increasing array of methods through which you can communicate with your prospective audience as a leader. These include telephone, emails, instant messaging, social media methods, and video calling e.g. Skype.

You, like almost everyone else probably has a preferred method. And the tendency is to choose that way of communicating with other people, every time.

When I carried out projects in different organisations, one of the most fascinating things for me was trying to learn the preferred means of communication for the different people I needed to work with. For some, I would send a raft of emails with virtually no response, then take a quick stroll to their office for a ten-minute chat and get all the answers I required and more. For others, getting to see them was nigh on impossible, yet if I called and left them a voicemail message, the same person who couldn't spare ten minutes for a face-to-face chat was prepared to call me back and spend half-an-hour discussing with me.

So I learnt that adaptation to others' preferred communication method was a significant key to enhancing my effectiveness. You may find it will do the same for you too.

Pursue resonance – My first exposure to the principle of resonance happened in my physics class in secondary school, many moons ago. Two similar tuning forks were held a bit of a distance away, but facing towards each other on a table. The base of one of the forks was struck against the table, which made it start vibrating. This vibrating fork was then held against the table and its sound muted, whilst we watched what would happen to the other tuning fork a short distance away.

To the amazement and delight of all the kids in the class (myself included), the second fork began to vibrate in tune with the first fork and gave out a ringing sound. The teacher announced to us that we had just witnessed sympathetic vibration or resonance.

The explanation for this is that vibratory bodies respond to other bodies that vibrate at a frequency very close to or equal to theirs.

You also experience resonance when your glass windows begin to rattle in response to the vibration of a passing truck or when a trained operatic singer shatters a glass cup with the power of her voice. The glass components are simply resonating with the harmonic frequency of the singer's voice.

The one thing that is common to all these scenarios is that ***nothing happens until the frequencies match***.

Understanding this is critical to becoming more effective in your communication as a leader. Knowing your purpose for communicating and what you want to share is good. Knowing the purpose of your audience and what they want to hear is good. But until the frequencies match… nothing happens.

Another thing that is common to the scenarios is that when the frequencies match, something inevitably happens… you simply cannot stop it.

Expanding your skill as a communicator therefore, entails the pursuit of resonance. This means that you become more focused on the actual results that you generate, than simply on the act of communicating.

For example if you are a community leader, your effectiveness in communication is not measured by your oration and the cheers you get after you speak. It is measured by the actual positive action that your hearers undertake as a result of having heard you.

As a parent, my communication with my daughter is not measured by the fact that I have given instructions for her to tidy up her room (I can hear the sighs of many parents here), I have achieved resonance when I walk into a tidy room that my child has lovingly cleaned up without further promptings from me.

Based on that last example, I guess I know that I have to keep working on improving my communication skills.

As a leader, you do have to improve how you craft your message and your delivery to your audience continually, and in a way that achieves resonance and delivers action to fulfil your mutual objectives.

Your secondary audience – One of the critical things to bear in mind is that you always have two types of audience.

a) Primary audience – the person(s) to whom you are communicating directly

b) Secondary audience – Other people who may be indirect recipients of your communication either with or without your blessing

With the rapid expansion of technologies and the emergence of new forms of media, it appears that the word 'confidential' is fast becoming obsolete. The Wikileaks scandal of 2010, only served to accentuate this fast growing phenomenon. WikiLeaks acquired over 250,000 U.S. State department diplomatic cables and published some of them in November 2010, to the consternation of the United States government and other governments around the world that were the subjects of those cables.

Therefore, whenever you communicate whether in writing or in person, always remember that there is a potential secondary audience. Craft your communications in a way that minimises the consequences should your communications reach unintended recipients. As someone once said, "You are always on the air."

4. Resource management capabilities

A key benefit of leadership is that it attracts increased resources. For example, as you become a higher quality leader in your organisation, you earn promotion, which often comes with an increased financial budget, a greater number of staff resources to handle, and other increasing responsibilities.

The challenge is that for many emerging leaders, this often becomes a burden because they have not been equipped to manage these higher-level resources.

Of course, not being properly equipped manifests itself in the mismanagement of those resources, which then diminishes the leadership influence of the erstwhile leader. This vicious cycle is repeated in thousands of ways across the landscape of leadership in organisations around the world.

I became the leader of one of the social clubs in my university, but found that my leadership would have come to a grinding halt most prematurely, if I had not recognised the need to manage the club's financial resources properly. I was not directly responsible for handling the finances, another club official was, and we agreed that no disbursements would be made without my sign-off.

One day, I made an impromptu request to check the financial records of the club and discovered to my chagrin that some funds had been paid out without my knowledge. I had an urgent meeting with my colleague and gave an ultimatum; the funds back within two days, or I would escalate the matter beyond his wildest imaginations. The funds were paid back pronto and we resolved the matter.

In retrospect, the amount involved was relatively small and the funds were used for a seemingly legitimate purpose, so why the fuss? If I had allowed that one instance to go unchallenged, I would have negated the financial management arrangements of the club and my ability to lead would be significantly diminished.

My colleague, although unhappy with me at the time of the incident, later told me that I had earned his respect as a result of my robust handling of that matter, more than probably anything else I had done as leader of the club until then.

There are many organisations that implode simply because of accusations or actual mismanagement of the financial resources. Sometimes the leader was not involved in any acts of corruption, they simply had abdicated responsibility for managing the finances to someone else and been stung by this mistake.

Simply put, you have to learn how to manage the resources that are attracted to you as a leader. If you are 'mathematically challenged' and view working with numbers as a fate worse than death, I can only say, "Sorry, the buck still stops with you." By all means, secure the assistance of professionals who are experts with numbers, but you do have to learn to understand the headline figures so that you know what is going on. There are many books that teach finances for non-finance people, study these materials to enhance your competency in this area.

Strategic Competences – Interactive Exercise

How do you demonstrate the quality of strategic thinking?

_____

_____

_____

What areas do you need to improve upon to raise your level of strategic thinking?

(And how will you do this?)

_____

_____

_____

On a scale of 1 to 10 (1 = lowest; 10 = highest), how would you rate your ability to handle crises? (And what do you need to raise your competency level?)

_____

_____

_____

What are the benefits of crises to you?

_____

_____

_____

On a scale of 1 to 10 (1 = lowest; 10 = highest), how would you rate your ability to communicate effectively?

_____

_____

_____

What areas of communication ability do you need to improve upon? (And how will you undertake the improvements?)

_____

_____

_____

Are you equipped to manage higher-level resources? (If NO, what steps will you take to address this?)

_____

_____

_____

Building Your Team

Success in achieving your vision or dreams will demand not just the application of your own continuously refined and improved, unique capabilities, it will demand that you marshal the collective efforts of other people and build a team to support the attainment of those dreams. The team may undertake their work in a location that is in close proximity to you, or it may be a virtual team that criss-crosses several continents and several time zones.

As Oren Harari stated, "Even a compellingly articulated vision only gets you so far. Great people are the key." This reinforces the perspective that leadership is the capacity to inspire worthy contributions from others towards the fulfilment of a noble endeavour.

If you desire to achieve results through a team, you are likely to encounter two types of contribution from anyone who joins your team.

1. Contractual contribution

This is the contribution from staff, colleagues, clients, or other stakeholders that is activated by 'contractual' obligations.

This is based on a quid pro quo arrangement, in which you provide some value e.g. a salary or other payment for which the recipient is obligated to provide some value in return.

For such an arrangement, most people only do just enough to ensure the maintenance of their obligation. E.g. the employee may do just enough not to get fired or the supplier may provide goods at the minimum acceptable level of quality.

Many leaders often enjoy only this type of contribution from their stakeholders and so they often have to resort to threats (of removing their side of the obligation) or manipulations i.e. pretending they will provide more of the expected payments in return for increased contributions from the stakeholders.

This form of contribution often leads to a working arrangement that is dry, devoid of joy for participants, and the results are transient or short-lived. The level of performance may rise for a short while but it will inevitably dwindle to the average performance that the contributors can get away with.

I refer to leaders who use contractual contributions as their primary source of results as pseudo-leaders.

2. Discretionary contribution

This is the type of contribution that your team members do not have to give. They are not obligated either by their legal contract or in any way whatsoever, to render this support. They are at total liberty to choose whether to give or to refuse giving the contribution without any adverse consequences to them whatsoever.

BUT... they choose, at their own discretion, individually or collectively, to give the support or contribution you require. It is a form of contribution that is activated by INSPIRATION.

The results are longer lasting, the stakeholders are positively energised, and their level of performance far outstrips what you can get from contractual contributions.

Long after the leader has left, his influence on the participants is still felt as a positive, enriching experience.

Leaders who evoke discretionary contributions have learnt how to create resonance with their teams. Such leaders focus on delivering results by aligning the worthy aspirations of their stakeholders with the achievement of their own noble goals.

I refer to such leaders as **inspirational leaders**. Through coaching, guiding, and mentoring, often done very subtly, you can help each member of your team to tap into their own personal greatness, and in so doing, engage a level of performance that is truly astounding.

In the past, I have tried both forms of leadership and with the benefit of experience, have learnt that inspirational leadership will leave you less fatigued, get you better results, improve your outcomes and reward you in unimaginable ways.

One main issue is that there is sometimes a tension between forcing contractual contributions and inspiring discretionary contributions, especially when you are facing a deadline or are under pressure of some other kind.

Whilst the use of contractual obligations will sometimes be necessary, great leaders consistently generate their results from the voluntary, discretionary contributions that the leaders inspire in their team, over and above the contractual obligations. The key to your increased effectiveness as a leader will be to learn how to activate the discretionary or voluntary contributions of your team, so that it becomes the default way of leading.

The following ideas will assist in building the high performance team that will support the fulfilment of your vision:

Cultivate strong empathetic relationships

Strong relationships are the foundation of organisational success. The quality of the contributions of each of your team members is directly related to the strength of their relationship with you. Weak relationships breed weak, lower quality contributions, whilst strong relationships galvanize strong, higher quality contributions.

You have to be intentional about cultivating these relationships. The saying, "People don't care how much you know until they know how much you care." is a powerful truth to embrace in your quest to build a high performance team.

The first step towards growing such strong empathetic relationships is the recognition that you are an emotional being and more often than not, your decisions and actions are driven by an emotional trigger. If you are in a negative state of mind such as anger, low self-esteem, or stress, you may find yourself lashing out at people for seemingly inconsequential reasons.

If you are in a positive state of mind such as confident or relaxed, you often find that you respond differently to the same situations that would have made you lash out before. It is therefore important to become more self-aware and learn how to adjust and control your emotional state.

The second step is to recognize that your team members are also emotional beings and everything you do impacts on their emotional core either directly or indirectly. Just as you respond to emotional triggers, so do your team members. Therefore, it is important to become highly aware of the emotional state of your team members as you interact with them.

The principle of resonance that we covered when we discussed effective communication is particularly critical for developing strong relationships.

Seek to understand your team members to establish at what frequency they are operating, as part of your interaction. The broad range of frequencies that I look out for when engaging with people are:

❖ Strongly negative – Would say no to whatever my request is. Relationship repair is required.

❖ Mildly negative – Predisposed to say no but would be open to at least, hear my proposals.

❖ Neutral – No opinions formed. Is neutral about me or my ideas but could easily swing either way.

❖ Mildly positive – Is generally predisposed to say yes to me and my ideas and give me the benefit of the doubt. We have built some positive rapport.

❖ Strongly positive – Would say yes to my request. We have a strong relationship and they trust me.

Based on an assessment of the team member's emotional frequency, you can then calibrate your interaction accordingly.

I would recommend also that your interaction should include a rapid feedback loop, which enables you to correct your assessment of the emotional frequency. What I mean is that if you approach an interaction with the expectation that the other party is on a strongly positive frequency, but they instead respond on a negative frequency, do not become negative in response to them. It simply means you have not achieved resonance and it is your responsibility as the leader to achieve this. Recalibrate your expectations and adjust your interactions to accommodate this new reality.

Applying this principle has often led to work colleagues in the past wondering what it would take to make me lose my positive disposition. I rarely ever did, because I understood the principle of resonance in cultivating my relationships and working with different stakeholders.

Have fun

An environment that is devoid of fun is one that is also devoid of positive energy, and an environment devoid of positive energy drains the physical and mental health and vitality of both you and your team members. In contrast, creating a working environment that includes a healthy dose of fun reduces organisational stress and increases productivity.

Sir Richard Branson, the billionaire owner of the Virgin Group says this about having fun, "it's important that people in business make sure the people working for them have fun. Business leaders take things far too seriously. They forget that people spend most of their lives at work, and it should be fun." [9]

Social researchers have identified that one of the best ways to predict the health and success of an organisation is how much fun the people are having whilst at work. Adrian Gostick and Scott Christopher in their book, *The Levity Effect: Why It Pays to Lighten Up* stated that, "An increasing body of research demonstrates that when leaders lighten up and create a fun workplace, there is a significant increase in the level of employee trust, creativity and communication, leading to lower turnover, higher morale and a stronger bottom line..."[10]

So, having fun in the workplace is not a frivolity to be avoided, or a waste of time. If you are serious about maximising the performance of your team, look again at the benefits to you of injecting lots of fun into your team's activities:

- ❖ Increased creativity – which means problems get solved faster and results come quicker.

- ❖ Greater trust between team members.

- ❖ Better communication – which reduces misunderstandings and tension.

- ❖ Higher morale.

- ❖ Less stress and people cope better with work demands.

- ❖ People feel more valued.

❖ Significantly reduced lateness, sick leave, or absenteeism – because they enjoy coming to work.

❖ Greater productivity.

❖ Increased profits or outcomes for your organisation.

Loyalty

Superlative performance is one of the products of loyalty to a leader, or the cause that the leader espouses. However, loyalty is not unidirectional. This means that it is not something that you demand from members of your team. Loyalty is tri-directional; it goes sideways (to peers), upwards (to senior team members) and downwards (to junior team members).

There are some leaders who attempt to trade-off loyalty for one stakeholder against loyalty to another one e.g. loyalty to the boss against loyalty to their junior team members. That is a losing proposition because your team will not be inspired to deliver consistently great results for a leader who is disloyal. And by the way, word will quickly reach the boss about your lack of loyalty, which will create a question mark in his mind about your true motives.

Loyalty is one of the components of integrity and people will go way above the call of duty to support you in achieving your goals, when they know that you are loyal to them.

Mentorship

Just as it is crucial for you to connect with the right kind of mentor in order to facilitate your continued growth as a leader, it is also crucial for you to be the right kind of mentor who will support the growth and development of your team members, because your real success as a leader is measured by the quality of leaders you develop.

Be willing to share your insights, values, secrets to success, and other resources that would help your team members emerge as high-quality leaders. This helps to strengthen your relationship with your team, enhances their productivity, and ultimately, could help them become the pool of talent from which you draw the core leaders to whom you will hand over the baton of leadership of your team or organisation.

Mentorship demands a sacrifice of time and effort, and sometimes, other additional resources, but it is well worth it. It is one of the most profound ways in which you demonstrate your belief in others.

You will reap the satisfaction of seeing someone develop and release their own greatness. You may also find that your mentee is in a position to help you in the future or that their accomplishments may just make you look good. For example, Tiger Woods, the golfing legend made his father, Earl Woods, who taught him how to play the game at an early age, look good.

Understand their personalities

Every person you meet is different and has their own unique strengths, capabilities, preferences, and emotional make-up. Take the time and effort to obtain deep insight into the different motivations that drive your team members and an appreciation for why they behave the way they do.

Seeking to understand their personality make-up is beneficial for two reasons.

1) You are better able to match tasks and responsibilities to their personality. There are some people who would go stir crazy if you gave them a job that demanded staying in an office, in front of a computer for long periods of time. Giving them a job that did not have this drawback would make them ecstatic.

   In contrast, there are other people who absolutely love the kinds of jobs where they would spend hours on end at their computers, analysing, and researching etc. Matching them to the right types of jobs brings alignment between their personalities and their daily work, which will serve to increase their productivity.

2) You are better able to engage with them, offer the rewards that are meaningful to them and stimulate their contribution to your team efforts because you understand what motivates them.

Learn what makes each member of your team tick and play to their strengths.

Cultural sensitivity

The world has become a global village with advances in transport and communications technology making it easier to interact with people from many cultures, perspectives, faiths, and experiences on a daily basis.

An effective leader must come to terms with this reality and appreciate that most people you will deal with have a different take on life from you. You therefore need to develop a heightened awareness and sensitivity to the different cultures of the people who may be part of your team. You will also need to cultivate a flexible attitude that enables you to respond effectively to the cultural differences that you encounter. Ultimately, it is about respecting every individual person because he or she matters as a human being.

The cultural differences may be based on language, religion, or values so it is important to pay attention to any differentiating factor between you and any other member of your team and incorporate this into every element of your interactions where possible.

One of the leadership failures of some western governments such as the USA and the UK has been to ignore the spiritual and cultural values of developing nations. They attempted to impose their own values on sexuality on some developing nations, threatening to withdraw development aid if those nations did not accept the western values. This resulted in a major backlash from some of those nations who viewed it as cultural imperialism and would rather remain true to their own spiritual and cultural values than succumb to what they considered an offensive imposition by western countries.

Business leaders have also fallen foul of the lack of cultural sensitivity and examples abound of such miscalculations.

In 2005, the fast food giant McDonald's rolled out a new television advert aimed at Chinese consumers, which showed a Chinese man kneeling before a McDonald's vendor and begging him to accept his expired discount coupon. However, begging is considered a shameful act in Chinese culture so, inevitably the advert caused uproar, and McDonalds had to withdraw it.

Just as governments and businesses are falling foul of a lack of cultural sensitivity, individuals are doing the same, often through ignorance. This has in some way contributed to the increasing array of legislation regarding equality and diversity that is showing up in many nations as a way of addressing some of the problems that may arise as a result of cultural insensitivities.

I remember attending a conference in the USA sometime ago, where most of the delegates were Africans resident in the USA. One delegate was Asian and a few were from the Caribbean. Most of the Africans resorted to speaking in their native dialects through much of the first two days, thereby excluding the Asian and Caribbean delegates from any meaningful participation in the conversations.

One of the conference leaders realised what was happening and had to make a public announcement to address the problem. A few weeks after that conference, I was attending an event in London where most of the attendees were Indian and there were very few non-Indians.

Again, the same problem arose and most of the non-Indians, including yours truly, felt excluded from meaningful conversations.

My point about these is that the perpetrators were not being deliberately malicious, nor were they actively seeking to exclude those who were different. They simply had not trained themselves to develop the sensitivity to cultural differences that would enable them to engage effectively with the diversity of attendees at those events.

As a leader, pay very close attention to cultural differences when you engage with other people within your team or outside it and seek to demonstrate the right attitude that reflects your awareness and respect for those you meet.

Optimism

In the natural course of pursuing your vision, you will encounter situations that attempt to throw you off course. There will be days when things don't go according to plan. At such times, you are called upon to exercise perhaps the most incredible power available to you and every other human... the power of choice... to choose the attitude with which you will respond to the unfolding circumstances.

You can choose an uplifting, energetic attitude filled with optimism and enthusiastic belief that you have what it takes within you, to overcome the situation you face, or you can choose a defeated, pessimistic attitude that saps you of the emotional fortitude required to be victorious.

Dr Susan Vaughan who has undertaken research on the power of optimism stated that, "Optimism has little to do with external reality, and everything to do with our ability to regulate our own inner world. It is the perception of being in control, not the reality that really matters."[11] It is therefore important to reiterate this truth... optimism or pessimism is a choice you make. It is not determined by your circumstances.

Unfortunately, many people exercise this choice in a way that creates a downward spiral for them. They choose to be become pessimistic and negative in their outlook, which makes it even more difficult to overcome their challenge and emerge from whatever the situation is that they are facing.

As a leader, you are called upon to choose a nobler alternative that not only lifts you up from mental or emotional doldrums, but also inspires your team to be lifted from any depths of negativity. You are required, in essence, to be the torchbearer for the flame of enthusiasm and optimism.

Have you heard the following statement made about someone? "He brightens up a room... just by walking out of it." That captures the impact of a leader without optimism on the team. Pessimism or optimism is like a virus. It infects those with whom it comes into contact. The impact of a leader with a positive, optimistic attitude on her team is like bursts of rainfall that revitalizes grass that has been wilted by the winds of adversity.

Choosing to be optimistic and embedding a culture of optimism within your team has tremendous benefits. In a 2009 research conducted by US based investigators on nearly 100,000 women and published in the journal, *Circulation12*, their findings included that:

- ❖ Optimistic women had a 9% lower risk of developing heart disease.

- ❖ Pessimists had higher blood pressure and cholesterol.

- ❖ Optimists had a 14% lower risk of dying from any cause after more than eight years of follow-up.

- ❖ Cynical women were 16% more likely to die over the same eight-year timescale.

The lead researcher, Dr Hilary Tindle, concluded that, "The majority of evidence suggests that sustained, high degrees of negativity are hazardous to health."

The results of this research corroborate the findings of earlier work undertaken by a Dutch team, which showed that optimism reduces heart failure risk in men.

Your personal energy of optimism affects your health. However, your personal health as a leader is not a private matter. It gives a sense of confidence to your organisation and infuses the team with the possibility of your vision being accomplished; Energy is infectious.

This positive impact of optimism cannot be overstated. It is therefore essential for the leader to actively cultivate and demonstrate an attitude of optimism as a model for the team to follow and also encourage the team to imbibe the optimistic attitude as their default mindset. This will bring health to you and to your organisation.

There are two simple keys to maintaining your optimism.

1) Rehearse your dreams and vision regularly – Place the vision and objectives that your team are pursuing in a prominent place so that they will have a constant reminder of why all the work they are doing is worth it. Seize every opportunity to remind them of their value to you and the organisation, and communicate this in a vibrant way that resonates with your team members.

2) Stay active and keep moving forward – This is especially true when you have just experienced a setback, as the general preference is to sit back and lick your wounds. Do not fall prey to this temptation, because it will very quickly lead to inertia and eventual death of enthusiasm for the vision. Instead, adjust your plans, reset your goals, and keep moving forward. The energy of forward movement, coupled with your continuous

modelling of personal enthusiasm will yield great results. As Sir Winston Churchill once put it, "Success consists of *going* from failure to failure without loss of enthusiasm."

Focus on productivity

In order to manage an organisation well, the leader needs to understand how to maximise the productivity of the team. This is accomplished by ensuring synergy between each component members so that the sum of the whole is bigger than the sum of the individual parts. Some simple ideas will help you raise the productivity level of your team.

Define clear productivity measures – As the saying goes, you can't hit a target you don't have. Similarly, if you don't set clear, measurable, productivity targets for your team, all you will get is people showing up each day on the treadmill of organisational activity, spending time and resources on non-essential activities, which do not take you closer to your objectives as efficiently as possible.

I once read the annual appraisal reports of a member of staff I inherited when I joined an organisation. I was astonished to find that there was no specific measure of productivity, by which her work had been judged in the last three years.

Suffice to say she was a thoroughly unhappy team member who saw her job as just a pitiful merry-go-round with no hope of progression. We analysed her job together and came up with specific goals, by which we could measure whether she was making progress or not. Having something to aim for, rekindled her passion and creativity and she became a more valuable member of the team, offering ideas that helped improve her individual performance and by extension, the team's results.

Let each member of your team know exactly what they are supposed to deliver and how it will be measured.

Monitor results – Always remember this mantra, "Inspect what you expect." Have a mechanism for tracking the performance of all team members by results. I would emphasise that the results should be tied to the achievement of your team's measurable objectives. I also emphasise the need to monitor for results, because experience has shown that increased activity may not necessarily equate to improved results.

As much as possible, link rewards (financial or otherwise) to results, otherwise you may get the perverse consequence of someone working hard, but delivering no demonstrable results worthy of the rewards or payment they receive.

Reward superlative performance – I believe that one of the greatest impediments to productivity in any organisation is a lack of direct correlation between rewards and performance. If you have set a goal as a leader and a member of your team has achieved the target, do not betray their trust by withholding the promised reward.

By the way, it does not matter if the qualifying team member is not your friend! Reward those who have earned it. Never deprive people of the rewards that they have earned, simply because there are areas of your mutual relationship you still need to work on. This is a matter of integrity for you as a leader that cannot be overemphasised.

Perhaps you have experienced this yourself? Or maybe you know someone who has? That sinking feeling in the pit of the stomach that comes when you have worked hard all year to earn your bonus or performance related pay or some other kind of reward (it could be an organisational award for example) and you are told that it would not be given to you.

Try as hard as you might, you simply cannot think of any justifiable reason why you did not receive your reward and the reasons given by the person who deprived you of your reward, sound so hollow that it is clear it was not based on any objective appraisal of your performance. I experienced this myself as a member of another club in my university days and I can assure you that it was a terrible feeling.

I have spoken to many people who have experienced similar things and the results are the same. Their commitment and passion for the organisation concerned went downhill from thereon, some, never to recover.

So, always reward extraordinary performance. It sends a clear signal to your team that you value outstanding contributions and motivates them to pursue the same.

Deal with underperformance – In the words of Dr Mike Murdock, "You cannot change what you tolerate." If you tolerate mediocre performance, you cannot expect superlative results. Have a mechanism within your team for addressing underperformance. Train, coach, mentor, and monitor any underperforming team member, so that they can raise their performance level. If all of these do not work, it may be that the team member is in a role that is unsuited to their unique capabilities. Consider reassigning such a team member to other suitable roles within your team or organisation.

If however, this does not yield results, it's time to help such a team member pursue other options outside your organisation. Do this graciously and allow them to leave with their dignity intact.

As tough as it sounds, it is absolutely necessary that you take these measures to protect your organisation against the cancer of non-productivity. If you don't, other team members will assume that you do not mind underperformance and will begin to emulate the underperforming team member, to the detriment of your goals and vision.

You simply have to be courageous and decisive enough to know when it's time to say, "thanks but goodbye."

Time management – I will not spend much time here talking about time management (no pun intended). I would simply say that a common characteristic amongst some of the greatest leaders in human history is the value that they place on time.

You have probably heard the saying that 'time is money'. That is not true. Time is more important than money.

Time is a finite gift that you have been given, which serves as the unit of exchange for everything else you ever hope to have, be, or do in your life. To be successful in business, you exchange time for learning, starting, and growing your business. To be successful in relationships, you invest time in meeting people, cultivating their friendships, and growing to know them more and more. To be successful in spiritual matters, you dedicate time towards the pursuit of spiritual truth and practices that bring you to your desired goal.

Place great value on your time by choosing carefully what you spend your time on. And educate your team about the value that you place on your time and theirs.

There are a myriad of time management courses that are available to assist you in improving how you maximise the use of your time. Find one that suits you, learn it, and apply it. And encourage your team members to do the same.

When all is said and done, time is all that you have. Time management is simply life management.

Solve problems fast – As you and your team work on the fulfilment of your objectives, situations arise that challenge your deadlines, challenge the harmony of your team, or even challenge the existence of your team or vision itself.

Regardless of the nature of the situation, one of the critical weapons in your arsenal as an effective leader is the capacity to solve problems fast. And this capacity rests on the attitude of decisiveness. As Brian Tracy once said, "Decisiveness is a characteristic of high-performing men and women. Almost any decision is better than no decision at all."

When your team require a decision, don't become a victim of paralysis by analysis, always evaluating, judging, thinking, but not providing a decision upon which they can act, and perhaps hoping that the situation would fade away if you just ignore it long enough. More often than not, the situation transitions into a problem, which if it is still left unresolved, turns into a crisis.

Yes, sometimes you may make a mistake, but being a real leader means that you are willing to make a decision despite the complexity or uncertainty of the situation you face. You use your best judgement to choose amongst your available options, based on clarity about your core values and overall goals and accept total responsibility for whatever the outcome of your decision may be.

Be encouraged by Anne O'Hare McCormick's observation that, "The percentage of mistakes in quick decisions is no greater than in long-drawn-out vacillation, and the effect of decisiveness itself 'makes things go' and creates confidence."

If you embrace all the above principles regarding building your team, I am convinced that you will be well positioned to build a high performance team that delivers results that far exceed your expectations. I have been privileged to apply these ideas to my own work with a variety of teams in different sectors and have been pleasantly rewarded with the high productivity teams that I am proud to have worked with.

Building Your Team – Interactive Exercise

Would your team follow you if their salary or other enticements were not available?

(This reflects the degree to which they feel inspired by your vision rather than the pay cheque.)

_____

_____

_____

Does your team only give their legal, contractual obligations and no more? (Or do they regularly give you their discretionary effort?)

_____

_____

_____

Consider the highest performing member(s) of your team. Do you know what really motivates them: their dreams, fears, aspirations, and expectations in working with you?

_____

_____

_____

Consider the poorest performing member(s) of your team. Do you know what really motivates them: their dreams, fears, aspirations, and expectations in working with you?

_____

_____

_____

Do you have alignment between the vision, objectives, and goals of your unit (business, department, team, or even family) with those of the individual members of the unit?

_____

_____

_____

Do you integrate fun into your working activities and that of your team? (If YES, describe how. If NO, why not? What do you need to improve in this area?)

_____

_____

_____

On a scale of 1 to 10 (1 = lowest; 10 = highest), how would you rate those who work with you in terms of their loyalty to you? (Why do you think it's so high/low?)

_____

_____

_____

On a scale of 1 to 10 (1 = lowest; 10 = highest), how would those who know you or work with you, rate you in terms of your loyalty to them?

(Why do you think it's so high/low?)

_____

_____

_____

Are you culturally sensitive as a leader? (How do you demonstrate this? In what ways could you improve?)

_____

_____

_____

On a scale of 1 to 10 (1 = lowest; 10 = highest), what is your personal optimism score as a leader? (How do you demonstrate this? In what ways could you improve?)

_____

_____

_____

On a scale of 1 to 10 (1 = lowest; 10 = highest), what score would (or do) the members of your team give you for optimism? (How does this differ from your own personal score? In what ways could you improve?)

_____

_____

_____

Do you demonstrate a focus on productivity, rather than just activity? (How and in what ways do you need to improve?)

_____

_____

_____

Do you manage your time effectively? (In what ways do you need to improve? What tools will you utilise to help you improve?)

_____

_____

_____

What other questions arise for you from this section?

_____

_____

_____

What will you do in response to these additional questions?

_____

_____

_____

Epilogue

Well friend, thank you for your time and the pleasure of your company as we journeyed together through the ideas in this book.

Wherever you turn, you can see the tragic effects of poor quality leadership. A sad description of the level of leadership that many of our communities and nations have to endure is captured by the following words of Tony Blair, the former prime minister of the United Kingdom:

> *"Leaders come in all shapes and sizes, and I have stumbled across the full range in my time. I recall sitting across the table from some leaders, unable to think of anything other than 'my God, the poor people of that country.' You get the dumb, the cynical, the tedious, the mildly unsuitable, the weird, the products of systems so mad and dysfunctional, you find yourself marvelling that the leader is sentient, let alone capable. And frankly, some weren't sentient."*[13]

Our world desperately needs a new breed of higher quality, visionary, principle-centred, competent, and courageous leaders who lead from the inside out. Our world needs you!

You are a quintessential original that embodies dreams, gifts, unique capabilities, and leadership potential that our world so desperately needs.

My hope is that something you have discovered in *The Leadership Jigsaw* has quickened something in you… perhaps an awareness or a decision to step up to your next level of effectiveness as a leader and to use some of the principles, methods, or ideas in this book as part of your toolkit for development.

If that is so, I rejoice greatly at the opportunity to have contributed in some small measure towards this phase of your journey. I urge you however, to go beyond decision… take action – Begin today and never stop.

Our world awaits all that you have to offer, and as you take the next step in your journey, my utmost desire for you is that you would dare to…

Unleash Your Leadership Genius… Release Your Greatness… !!!

Interactive Exercise

What are the three main commitments for your leadership development arising from reading 'The leadership Jigsaw?'

_____

_____

_____

What three things will you do over the next three/six months to expand your leadership ability?

_____

_____

_____

What other questions have arisen for you from your journey through The Leadership Jigsaw?

_____

_____

_____

What will you do in response to these additional questions?

_____

_____

_____

Notes

Vision

[1] Dr Munroe, Myles. Becoming a Leader (2009 edition).

[2] Eva LaGallienne, quoted in Leadership when the heats on by Danny Cox with John Hoover (2002).

Responsibility

[3] Dr Myles Munroe. Becoming a Leader (2009 Edition).

[4] James M. Kouzes & Barry Z. Posner. The Leadership Challenge, 2002, Pg 27.

Integrity

[5] Oren Harari (2002), Leadership Secrets of Colin Powell.

[6] Warren Bennis, On Becoming a Leader (xxxiii, xxvii).

[7] John F. Kennedy, words in his speech of 22/11/63, the day he was assassinated.

Personal Growth

[8] Pastore R S (http://teacherworld.com/potdale.html accessed 27/05/13).

Building Your Team

[9] From interview with Christine Lagorio quoted in http://www.inc.com/articles/201112/sir-richard-branson-stop-taking-business-so-seriously.html; accessed on 12/11/12.

[10] Adrian Gostick and Scott Christopher quoted in http://career-advice. monster.com/in-the-office/workplace-issues/fun-at-work-matters-levity-effect/article.aspx; accessed on 12/11/12.

[11] Dr Susan C. Vaughan (2000). Half Empty, Half Full: Understanding the Psychological Roots of Optimism.

[12] Reported in BBC News website, http://news.bbc.co.uk/1/hi/health/8193180. stm; accessed on 13/11/12.

Epilogue

[13] Tony Blair Quoted in TIME magazine of 13/09/10.

What Other Leaders are Saying...

The Leadership Jigsaw is one of the very best books I have read on Leadership in a long time. Yemi captures the heart of true leadership and skilfully helps the reader break free of the chains that hold you back from being the best leader you can be.

Whether from bad to good or from good to great, the practical ideas and principles in this book will radically transform you into a better quality leader.

If you lead a business, a home, or any enterprise, or you aspire to do so, I highly recommend that you don't walk, run to get *The Leadership Jigsaw*, read it, and apply its message to your life. You will be exceedingly glad you did, as I am.

Bill Walsh - CEO Powerteam International

America's Business Expert and Author of 'The Obvious.'

In "*The Leadership Jigsaw*," Yemi highlights key leadership issues including having a bigger vision, focus and being in the driver's seat of your life... knowing where you wish to go and how you wish to succeed. An interesting read. I found this book both delightful and refreshing.

Darshana Ubl

Entrepreneur, keynote speaker and award-winning SME business advisor.

Leadership is the one phenomenon in life that continues to make or break our world, depending on who is doing the leading. From the beginning of time, there has been a struggle between good leaders and bad leaders which has continued to produce war, malice, and corruption in governments, nations, communities, businesses and families.

When one thinks of jigsaws, one thinks about many different, oddly shaped pieces with a variety of different edges and grooves that when placed correctly and together in their respective posts or functions produces the positively desired results. *"The Leadership Jigsaw"* does exactly that for the leader who endeavours to be an excellent leader in any and every arena of life. It is a practical manual that includes practical advice and examples aimed at providing a balanced approach of the multiple characteristics to true, quality leadership.

As a leader in my own right and in my own area of expertise, I understand that I don't know it all and I am aware of the importance of constantly sharpening my knowledge, skills, and abilities in order to increase the level and quality of my influence in the world at large.

I especially and highly recommend *"The Leadership Jigsaw"* to every young person to make it a part of your library. Whether you own a business or desire to own and run a business of your own someday, this is for you. It doesn't matter who you are or where you came from, if you have a heart to do something that will change the world, your leadership has begun. Start here!!!

Charisa Munroe

Vice President – Myles Munroe International

The Leadership JIGSAW resolves the CRISES in Leadership worldwide - Yemi has created the MUST READ fresh tools to turn leadership crises into leadership abundance. Take this tool kit to every CEO and department head worldwide. I so approve of this message.

Berny Dohrmann

Chairman/Founder – CEOSPACE

This is an inspirational leadership book detailing the tools, information, processes and strategies to become an effective leader of the 21st Century. I highly recommend it.

Dr Dayo Olomu

Vice Chair, Chartered Institute of Personnel Development – South London

Corporate Trainer, and Motivational Speaker, Business Transformation Strategist.

The Leadership Jigsaw is a must read for every front-line leader! Yemi Akinsiwaju shares insights that inspire readers to make a bigger difference in their own homes, workplaces, and immediate society. Yemi shows that collectively, we can change the world for the better.

I urge you to self-reflect, self-assess, and to then, self-correct through applying Yemi's prescriptions for effective leadership and you will be well equipped to accelerate your success and bring positive transformation to your world.

Dr Rich Schuttler

Former Dean - School of Advanced Sciences, University of

Phoenix, Arizona, USA

Founder and CEO, Organization Troubleshooter, LLC

As you and I know there's an enormous gap between leadership and mere management. In every aspect of life more, more-effective leaders are urgently needed. But where to find them?

Now with Yemi Akinsiwaju's '*The Leadership Jigsaw*' - managers and those who are managed can become powerful, persuasive, passionate leaders.

Starting with the concept of self-leadership, Yemi explores the myths and misconceptions of leadership and goes on to clearly explain not only what needs to be done but how to do it.

I loved the question sessions at the end of each chapter. They are a perfect way to take the numerous learnings and easily embed them.

If you're looking to be a leader of yourself, a leader of people or a leader of a successful organisation then Yemi's '*The Leadership Jigsaw*' is your next must read.

If you're involved in any organisation, commercial or not - this book MUST be in your organisation's library; better still - buy every member a copy.

As an avid reader for 60 years I've lost count of how many 100s of books I've read - suffice to say 'The Leadership Jigsaw' by Yemi Akinsiwaju - just made it into my top 10.

Go read it now.

Peter Thomson

CEO, Peter Thomson International

"The UK's leading strategist on business and personal growth"

The subject of leadership has been a fascination of mine since I was told I was a servant leader. At the time I was leading a community I had set up to support business owners. I did feel my role was to serve them and their needs. Since that time, in the 1990's, I have worked within many organisations and with a diverse group of people. Understanding what they want to achieve has always been of paramount importance to me, understanding their values and the shared values of the people within the teams I work with is critical to success.

I am not a managerial or operational Leader. I see things that need solving, I hold a vision of the new world where we now have a chance to be socially connected and build deep trust between us. I see that leadership styles are adapting to this social world. The autocratic leader is not a role model for modern business or institutions. Reading Yemi's book will be a revelation to many, it shares the deep values we should all hold in taking responsibility to lead others.

More and more people need to lead now. The growth of start-ups, the growth of 'leading a following' passes the responsibility to a much wider group of people. Yemi has done a great service in documenting the importance of leadership. Knowing 'thyself' is the first step, then, you can adapt, understand, and support others.

I highly recommend *The Leadership Jigsaw* to the leader or aspiring leader keen to expand on your knowledge of leadership and your ability to lead more effectively.

Penny Power OBE

Founder of Ecademy & Digital Youth Academy

Author of the bestselling book, 'Know Me, Like Me, Follow Me'

"Whether we like it or not, at some point in our lives we will be called up, nominated or forced to lead. This leadership demand may come about from a family, business or even a community situation. *'The Leadership Jigsaw'* is written in a very methodological and captivating way and gives you the essential, practical and inspiring steps to become an effective leader in any given situation; and it all starts with YOU."

Mac Attram

Co-founder & Director of SalesPartners UK

Business Coach, Trainer and Author

Acknowledgements

Every literary work is the product of many minds and this book is no different. It is the culmination of ideas learned from many teachers and leaders who have influenced me directly or indirectly. Such influences have been through their audio-visual material, their books, or the example of their lives.

For my many work colleagues, business associates, personal development enthusiasts, and leadership advocates through the years, thanks for the rich deposits of leadership insights and practices you have deposited in my life as our paths crossed, sometimes fleetingly and sometimes more enduringly.

To my beautiful wife, Abi, thank you for being my precious partner in our ongoing journey to deploy our leadership potential for the benefit of our generation and future ones. To my precious daughters, Seun, Tolu, and Tosin, I love you very much and thank you for your patience with me as I have sought to apply the lessons covered in this book to our lives and to enable me to become a more effective leader in our home.

I express my profound love and gratitude to my parents, Emmanuel and Grace Akinsiwaju who, through your personal example have instilled in me a passion to seek truth and live with love and integrity, the cornerstones of true leadership.

To my mentor, Dr Myles Munroe, thanks for all that you are, which speaks much louder than all that you have done to assist many millions around the world to discover, release, and maximise their leadership potential, through the pursuit of their personal purpose. Your passion for truth, commitment to wisdom, love, and your constant encouragement has borne more fruit in motivating me to produce this book.

To you, the reader, I commend your desire to pursue insights and ideas that will enable you to live more effectively and release the leadership greatness within you to enrich humanity. Thank you for choosing '*The Leadership Jigsaw*' as one of the tools to assist you in your journey.

Finally, to the epitome of the purest and transcendent form of leadership, God almighty… thank YOU!

About the Author

YEMI AKINSIWAJU, known as the Leadership Catalyst is the founder and CEO of DaySpring Consulting UK, a leadership consultancy dedicated to enhancing the leadership capacity of individuals and organizations.

Yemi is also a trustee of the International Third World Leaders Association (ITWLA), an organisation devoted to training and developing leaders in over 80 developing nations.

Yemi is a multi-gifted international speaker, business consultant and author, focussed on the crucial issues of leadership, personal transformation, organisational effectiveness, social and spiritual development. He is the author of the highly acclaimed book, *Scorecard: Achieving Success and Balance in a Turbulent World*.

He has addressed audiences from over 50 nations as a conference speaker, seminar facilitator, mentor, trainer, coach and in television and radio appearances.

You can visit him on www.YemiAkinsiwaju.com

Share Your Thoughts

I am always keen to expand my leadership insights and recognise that you have wisdom that may represent a different perspective from what I have shared in the Leadership Jigsaw, so please drop me a line to share your thoughts.

Also, in writing this book, I have sought to contribute to the expansion of your leadership consciousness, capacity or capability. I sincerely hope that I have being able to accomplish one or more of these objectives. I look forward to hearing from you about how *The Leadership Jigsaw* has contributed to your leadership journey.

You can reach me via:

Email: Yemi@YemiAkinsiwaju.com

Website: www.YemiAkinsiwaju.com

Other Resources

Scorecard: Achieving Success and Balance in a Turbulent World

"An Inspirational read...Simply a mind-set shifter for steady success and fulfilment."

Amal Simothy FCCA

(Entrepreneur and Co-Founder of AccountingPreneur)

"This has to be one of the best and inspiring books that I have read in the last 2-3 years. I have a new spark for life and a greater zeal to succeed in all that I do. I will give the book to people I meet who express a genuine desire to move from being good to great and are willing to be stretched in all areas of their lives to achieve their goals."

Mike Smith

(Award-winning Metropolitan Police Officer and Founder of Word for Weapons)

Available from Amazon.com and other good bookstores

www.ingramcontent.com/pod-product-compliance
Lightning Source LLC
Chambersburg PA
CBHW060314220326
41598CB00027B/4323